nature in design

ALAN POWERS

1887: Willow Boughs

... Remember Nature – as
she appeared indoors? Not mirror-to-face
but somehow conventionalised perforce.

Now draw that outside in again
for the walls enclosing men and women,
and so confirm that what comes in

has been transformed. And you remember
Nature, how she proceeds? December
cold, March fresh, June hot, September

mellow – by change? Those are the words:
Transform, Change. And afterwards
remember the word Beyond that guards

all wonderlands. So. Here is Nature
conventionalised: this pattern on paper
outrunning time, as More's Utopia

raced the henrician state of things:
here is Change, the happenings
mind has submitted to the process, Think

At workday's ending, close the door
and settle. What a design is for
adds definition to the natural law

of, say, these willow boughs – strange
new forms of life, a legend's changeling
substituted, rearrangement.

Remember Nature, how she is human?
son, daughter, man, woman
and all the promise each might summon?

Transform, Change. O let the Arts
take hold, and tip the world on its arse
and here goes! Beyond comes to pass!

From Morris Papers by Arnold Rattenbury, published by
Shoestring Press in 1996, the centenary of the death of
William Morris. The poems in the book refer alternately to
William Morris's writings and his wallpaper designs.
'Willow Boughs' is illustrated on page 97 of this book.

nature in design

ALAN POWERS

conran
OCTOPUS

To my mother

Half-title page: Arum lily (*Zantedeschia aethiopica*).
Title page: Hat by Philip Treacy, Autumn/Winter 1998.
Opposite: Section through a nautilus shell.

First published in 1999 by
Conran Octopus Limited
a part of the Octopus Publishing Group
2–4 Heron Quays
London E14 4JP

Commissioning Editor Stuart Cooper
Project Editors Paula Hardy and Christine Davis
Copy-editor Chris Bessant
Proof-reader Gwen Rigby
Creative Director Leslie Harrington
Designer Peter Avery
Picture Research Ally Ireson and Claire Taylor
Production Controller Sue Sharpless

British Library Cataloguing-in-Publication Data
A catalogue record for this book is available from the British Library

ISBN 1 84091 046 1

Colour origination by Sang Choy International, Singapore
Printed in China

contents

'Nature' and 'design' are two words whose meaning is much contested, although we use them all the time and think we know what they mean. The critic Raymond Williams referred to 'nature' as 'perhaps the most complex word in the language', and 'design' is scarcely less so. These words are difficult because they each mean more than one thing, and because everyone's world is directly affected by both of them, whether they like it or not. Perhaps by putting the two ideas into conjunction, like using one chemical to test another, we shall find out more about each. The links between nature and contemporary design are obvious in many ways. We could go into a department store and choose furnishing fabrics with flower patterns, or plain fabrics made from natural fibres. There will be floor coverings made from

nature in design: an introduction

rushes or jute, furniture made from solid wood (from sustainable forests, of course), pure cotton clothes without 'synthetics', 'ecological' detergents or washing powders and energy-saving light-bulbs. In the food hall, we could buy organic apple juice, organic wholemeal bread or unpasteurised cheese, knowing that in every case we are getting closer to nature. At the same time, we know that these choices are made within a particular cultural context, conditioned by things we read and hear.

The way in which we have become self-consciously aware of our culture has, for many people, placed nature at a great distance. Yet as our shopping list shows, the rise of the ecological movement has made us ask a great many questions in our role as consumers, partly from altruism, partly for self-protection, and partly from a mixture of other motives, including pure enjoyment (in the case of food), sound economic sense (as with light-bulbs) and visual preference, which is seldom entirely separate from the opinion we wish other people to have of us. The sense of an impending ecological crisis is one of the newest factors to enter the field of design, and while it has already caused many changes, its implications are still being worked out.

Early in the 1960s, the design theorist Victor Papanek wrote that 'there are professions more harmful than industrial design, but only a very few of them'. His fellow American designers were outraged, but if what he said was true then, a great deal has already changed. It is easy to be an eco-pessimist, expecting the worst, but there are choices to be made between better and worse ways of confronting our plight. As the ecologist Jonathan Porritt has written: 'The only thing people are arguing about now is just how long we can go on living before the natural systems on which we depend simply crack up. The optimists say we have bags of time to get things sorted out; the pessimists wake up every morning half expecting to step out of bed straight into the final ecological abyss.'

The designer has a role not only in working actively to avoid this abyss but also in making design a delightful process rather than one of drudgery and deprivation. The pleasure of the eye, which ought to run through all design work, is itself formed by the habits of observing nature. In this way, nature can be the medium, the message and the material of design, breaking apart the dowdy mental furniture that constitutes so much of

Previous page
The maze at Longleat, Wiltshire, uses natural materials to model a whirlpool-like figure.
Below Power lines in Arizona. Electricity is a natural force, but our use of it may well destroy the natural environment.

'culture'. In the words of Ezra Pound:

Pull down thy vanity, I say pull down.

Learn of the green world what can be thy place

In scaled invention or true artistry …

The puzzle that remains in ecologically conscious design is one of appearances. In the 1970s, the ecological 'look' emerged as a reaction to everything machine-made, but a great many things that look like this are, in fact, the product of the most sophisticated industrial processes. Before the rise of industrialism, designers and craftsmen looked primarily to nature as a source of form, and produced objects that have always been highly valued for their beauty. There are plenty of examples to show that, while beauty and ecology are not automatically connected, they are certainly perfectly compatible.

In the more factual world of engineering and calculation, much can be learnt by analogy from the 'purposive structure' in nature – the way trees or birds are apparently 'designed' to perform their function with the greatest efficiency. The way in which nature appears to be 'designed' cannot fail to interest designers, scientists and even theologians, although the number of direct borrowings is surprisingly small. In engineering structure, the requirements for strength imposed by buildings, ships or aeroplanes are different from those found in nature, which seldom tries to resist torsional stress. Even so, nature and design are operating in related fields when trying to retain strength and decrease wind-resistance, while eliminating unnecessary structure.

Above The dandelion seed head is beautiful and functional at the same time.

We may therefore seek functional explanations for the things we find beautiful in nature, such as the colouring of a bird's feathers or the shape of an individual leaf. It is comforting to think that these things may not be gratuitous or arbitrary, even though we may not fully understand them. Both the passionate advocates of Charles Darwin's theory of natural selection and their opponents, the Creationists, seek a total explanation for a 'designed universe'. Nature, however, seems to be based neither on a game of Snakes and Ladders, where some win and some lose, nor on a completely preordained set of plans. Rather, it is based on a game in which the 'other side' keeps changing shape. As players, we are not allowed leave the field and become pure spectators. We have to guess what the rules are as the game goes along, without the benefit of a referee. Nobody ever wins, but the game goes on.

Discussion of this subject has increased greatly in recent years with scientific discoveries such as chaos theory, which really describes a higher form of order, and fractals, the forms in nature that exhibit the same pattern on different levels of scale. These have begun to alter our understanding of the structure of the universe. Not all these findings have a direct practical application – we cannot set

Above Patterns in nature: the shell of the tent olive (Olivia porphyria) found in Baja California.

fractals to work for us, although we can admire their complexity. However, they suggest ways in which the gap between art and science, which widened progressively during the middle years of the twentieth century, can be bridged by new structures of thought. The implications for designers may be less in the form of tangible things around us, and more in different organisational models and mental habits.

The peculiar task of the design professions is to work in the worlds of fact and fancy, separately or together. Things that we now call design have, throughout the history of humanity, also been important ways of understanding our place in the world, and this interpretive function of design can now be seen to be as important as the 'purposive' function. This accounts for what Terence Conran calls the 'magic ingredient' in design, which can be recognised but not quantified or produced mechanically on demand. Sometimes both functions act together, and it is tempting to seek a theory that connects one with the other, but the game of nature, which exhibits more patterns than our eyes can readily grasp, seems constructed to tease us.

nature and culture

Ecology and the popularisation of new science have done much to change current design, and the results can be seen not only in new products in the fields of fashion and interior design but also in student degree shows and design fairs, where new craftsmen and women first show their wares. Nature can provide a 'look' and a style to any designed object, but its potential is much greater. Fundamentally it offers a profound and satisfying understanding of ourselves and our place in the world, and the ability – through the practice of design – to answer certain questions that cannot be answered by the research scientists, the poets or the eco-campaigners.

Among the barriers to realising these possibilities are pieces of mental furniture representing our categories of 'nature' and 'culture'. These need to be brought out into the light and examined. The fact that good design and good food have been brought together so successfully in recent years gives an important clue. Although eating and design might appear to be quite independent activities, what we increasingly value in our comestibles is the natural goodness of the ingredients, and a treatment in the kitchen that enhances them without losing their individual qualities. There is more style, visual and gastronomic, in the kind of wholesome but refined simplicity pioneered by Alice Waters in her famous restaurant, Chez Panisse, in Berkeley, California, than in traditional haute cuisine. The experience goes beyond eating to become a statement about life and its relationships – something that not only feeds the physical body with proteins and other food products but also lifts the spirits and makes life seem better.

Nature and culture are useful opposites. If culture is defined as all those human activities that make us separate from nature, it follows that nature must decrease as culture increases. We may come to believe that we are completely outside nature, neither seeking nor trusting any messages that we seem to receive from it. The two possible positions can be typified by the poets William Wordsworth and Samuel Taylor Coleridge, both of whom did much to influence the English view of nature. Wordsworth saw nature as the source of our most profound insights:

One impulse from a vernal wood

May teach you more of man,

Of moral evil and of good,

Than all the sages can.

(*The Tables Turned*)

Coleridge, on the other hand, declared that it was all a projection:

… we receive but what we give,

And of ourselves alone does Nature live.

(*Dejection: An Ode*)

Coleridge was right to say that we cannot separate our view of nature from what we already know. But perhaps Wordsworth was also correct in thinking that there is something 'out there', and that our knowledge can develop and change in response to nature. Yet the Romantic movement encouraged an unrealistic standard of nature as something utterly separated from culture. Even today, some people conceive of nature only in terms of areas of the earth's surface which are apparently unaffected by humans, such as the American National Parks. But this is an extreme view, based on a belief that man himself is not a part of nature, and is incapable of working harmoniously with it.

In an urban society, nature sometimes seems, as Oscar Wilde suggested, entirely the creation of art – although not, perhaps, for those who are at close quarters with it, dealing with the effects of a flood or even just pulling up weeds. There are problems for everyone when the balance between nature and culture is upset. Becoming over-sentimental about nature is as bad as ignoring it or treating it like a machine. Many people are suspicious of the claims made by 'deep ecology', which seeks to subject all human activity to the laws and requirements of nature. While the crisis to which this attitude is a response is real enough, this type of solution seems to step outside our own place in the interaction, almost to demand the abolition of culture and anything it represents. It seems more like a tyranny than a liberation.

Is the natural the same as the good? We can decide only for ourselves, but even the most cynical may sense that our physical well-being ultimately requires us to recognise what our bodies tell us about our needs – for fresh air, sunlight, clean water and freedom from continuous mechanical noise. Much that is manufactured today feeds a kind of physical or mental addiction, brought on by a stimulus that is initially satisfying, but which requires frequent replenishment – be it fast food, recorded music or rapid travel. We are so afraid of boredom that we will often fail to take time to look nature in the face and discover ourselves.

Is nature boring? It can certainly seem so when presented as dead matter, as is often the case when the sciences are taught. The idea of living nature has been spoken of down the centuries by poets and visionaries, who were often dismissed as fantasists or madmen. However, it has recently acquired some well-informed and persuasive advocates. To the designer, the distinction is provable not by experiment but by the quality of the work, which may be inspired by nature in many different ways. It is not just a case of copying natural forms; rather it is a matter of getting inside the processes of nature and transforming them through the medium of the human mind, changing them without denaturing them.

Above A balance of nature and geometry creates magic at the chateau of Chenonceaux in the Loire Valley, France, built in 1515.

Nature can probably be found in some form in almost any piece of design. The depiction of fruit and flowers on textiles or in architecture is one obvious level of influence. However, the relationship can be more subtle, and the older or more 'primitive' the work we are looking at, the more subtle it is likely to be, involving not only a 'decorative motif', as a modern designer or historian might call it, but a complete view of the world.

It is possible to speak of a whole age, from the beginning of human creativity until the middle of the second millennium after Christ, in which traditional beliefs dominated the field we now call 'design'. In this context, 'traditional' refers not to a self-conscious tradition deriving from an individual or school,

a natural history of design

but to an awareness of the objectivity of the world; a sense of shared standards of excellence outside the realm of personal taste. Looking at non-western cultures even in quite recent times, we can see the importance of design and art as part of a traditional civilisation.

The modern distinction between design and art was not an issue in traditional civilisations, such as the Ottoman Empire, whose highly trained dyers were responsible for the medieval Turkish carpets. All objects had some quality of beauty and meaning, and although some were more purely useful than others, symbolic significance was also part of the function of everything. The distinction between the utilitarian and the purely aesthetic did not exist. Hence, for a traditional craftsman, any talk about the difference between nature and non-nature would simply be incomprehensible, although his approach to nature might vary from the naturalistic to the abstract.

There is, therefore, a paradox in discussing traditional arts in relation to the concepts of 'nature' and 'design'. Traditional civilisations might provide us with the most complete paradigms, but such people would not comprehend our attempts to categorise these concepts. However, an understanding that such separate categories can hinder our appreciation of nature's significance may give us insight into our contemporary situation and our search for a holistic understanding of ourselves and the world.

Previous page The Gothic style refined structure until, skeleton-like, it was as thin as it could afford to be for its load. **Below** Architects Birds Portchmouth Russum made this proposal in 1992 for the seafront at Morecambe, Lancashire. Giant 'shrimps' house seaside amenities.

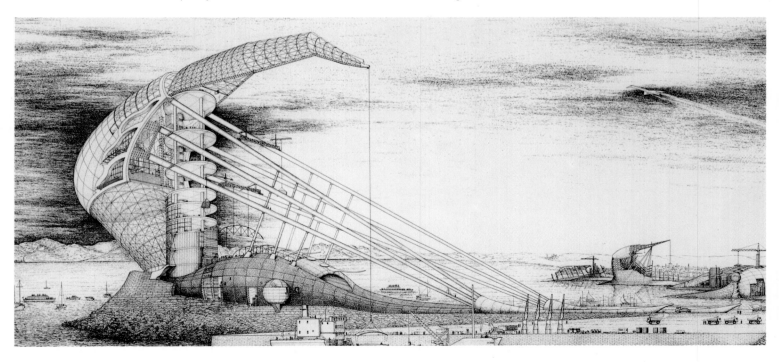

the transition from traditional arts

According to those who study the history of ideas, the foundations of European thought were laid in Greece some 2,500 years ago, with the emergence of a civilisation that is generally seen to represent mankind's transition from the 'traditional' world. Some ancient Greek works of architecture and sculpture, such as the Parthenon or the *Winged Victory*, are held up as models of perfection. Here nature is 'imitated' in the sense that its principles are understood and reproduced, a quality which arises from a real engagement with the world.

Above 'The objects in nature and the results of calculation are clearly and cleanly formed,' wrote Le Corbusier of the Parthenon, Athens, undoubtedly the most famous example of classical Greek architecture.

The art of the Middle Ages in Europe was deeply informed by a shared intuitive understanding of the meaning of the world. Chartres cathedral, rebuilt after a fire in the thirteenth century, contains many layers of geometric and symbolic relationships that date back to before Christianity. Some of the same density of reference can be inferred from the great abstract pavement laid by Italian craftsmen in Westminster Abbey, London, in 1268. Smaller details, such as the carvings in the chapter house at Southwell Minster in Nottinghamshire, from around 1330, show nature in a more familiar way, with recognisable plants beautifully rendered into architectural ornament. Christianity has been criticised for its tendency to consider natural beauty as a distraction from the spiritual life, but this danger is hardly apparent at Southwell, where many heads of 'Green Men', images of mankind in a state of nature, smile through the foliage.

Since the European Renaissance, art criticism has conventionally approved the 'naturalism' seen at Southwell as a superior form of truth. There are different kinds of truth, however. The gradual decline in awareness of the symbolic, religious and magical qualities of nature was, in one sense, the great achievement of the Renaissance. However, when we look at Leonardo da Vinci (1452–1519), it is hard to separate the art from the technology, or the science from the philosophy, in his stream of images and ideas.

The shift in attitudes to nature from the sixteenth century onwards is intimately bound together with the wider sphere of design – the diffusion through society of different ways of imagining, producing and marketing goods for commercial gain. Every kind of knowledge was brought to bear on the development of the material world, from double-entry book-keeping (a Renaissance invention that underlies the capitalist system) to faster ways of making cloth and turning metal.

In the history of ideas, the *Discourse on Method*, written in 1637 by the French thinker René Descartes (1596–1650), was an important point of departure. Descartes imagined a complete uprooting of all inherited knowledge and its replacement by a new structure, in which everything was rationally verifiable. The thought process began with a vision of a city built according to a uniform design, as opposed to one that has grown piecemeal. This is a perfect image of the 'modernist project', in which context and individuality are subordinated to regularity and universality. Descartes also made a division between the mind and the body, objectifying observed phenomena irrespective of the observer's influence on them.

Descartes was expressing an extreme version of an idea originating with Plato in ancient Greece: that there are two realities. One exists in the realm of pure thought, while the other is the world around us, which we can see and touch. The difference is that Plato gave credence chiefly to the first, while Descartes required the observable universe to furnish all the necessary information about reality. In practice, the secular physical world was a resource to be exploited for material benefits.

Descartes' philosophy had immediate consequences in the realm of design, challenging received wisdom from Plato about the inherent beauty of certain proportions and geometric figures. However, the effects were gradual, and it is only in the Modern Movement of the twentieth century that we find the fullest expression of his ideas.

In the seventeenth and eighteenth centuries, scientific discovery was still mixed with a capacity for wonder and delight, as seen in the Baroque and Rococo styles. Artists and designers responded to the irregularities of nature with curves and counter-curves. Imagery of animals, plants and rocks was frequently employed in symbolic and allegorical compositions, as in the fountains of Gianlorenzo Bernini (1598–1680) in Rome, which include tritons and elephants. Bernini's rival, Francesco Borromini (1599–1667) designed the tower of St Ivo in Rome in the form of a giant spiralling shell. The same exuberant fantasy was found in English silverware, with fantastic swirling shapes of shells and branches.

man and machine

The Industrial Revolution of the late eighteenth and early nineteenth centuries depended greatly on Descartes' separation of specialised areas of knowledge and experience. The old traditions of craft guilds gave way to impersonal relationships. Machines made craft skills less valuable and the 'division of labour' marked a new way of producing manufactured goods.

Right The Industrial Revolution brought improved living standards, but at a heavy cost to the environment, as shown in this print from the 1840s.

Industrialisation produced an alienation from nature that we are still working to resolve two hundred years later. This change seems to have taken place as much in people's minds as in outward physical conditions, favouring hard and verifiable information in place of intuition and feeling. William Blake (1757–1827), the English painter and poet, expressed the difference between the two states of mind succinctly: 'The tree which moves some to tears of joy is in the eyes of others only a Green thing that stands in the way. Some see Nature all Ridicule and Deformity ... & some scarce see Nature at all. But to the Eyes of the Man of Imagination, Nature is Imagination itself.'

The change from country to town living was a recognisable symptom of the modern condition. John Ruskin (1819–1900) wrote that a new urban-bred generation would find it difficult to achieve the kind of close personal contact with nature that he had enjoyed as a child: 'All vitality is concentrated through those throbbing arteries [the railways] into the central cities; the country is passed over like a green sea by narrow bridges, and we are thrown back in continually closer crowds upon the city gates.'

Town dwellers affirmed their rising social status by discarding their rural origins, yet the country was always physically near enough for contact with nature not to be lost completely. The Parisian working class could visit the riverside entertainment places depicted by the Impressionists, but even their pictures show factory chimneys in the background.

The painter John Constable (1776–1837) wrote of the influence on his art of his childhood memories: 'The sound of water escaping from mill-dams, etc., willows, old rotten banks, slimy posts and brickwork, I love such things.' It is interesting to note that Constable's affection was for the work of man in nature, which modifies nature's action in controlling the flow of the river, and is in turn modified by nature's action in causing decay. It is not only a visual memory: it also includes sound and, by implication, the whole range of sensations that Constable's paintings still evoke.

Above P. A. Rysbrack's painting of the gardens at Chiswick House, London (c.1728–30) shows the theatrical style of Baroque garden design, which gave way to a taste for greater naturalism.

The innocent enjoyment of everyday designs from Constable's lifetime is still available today, although such items as silver spoons, chairs, chests of drawers, dinner plates and teacups are now so highly esteemed as to place many of them beyond the reach of the modest collector. The quality of design from the period twenty years before and after the French Revolution of 1789 has long been upheld as the summit of good taste. From folk-art, which within its limited compass rarely makes mistakes of taste, upwards to the highest levels, there was a universal ability to judge proportion and scale, and to see the right place for ornament.

Was this connected with the evident pleasure in nature taken by all social classes? The weavers who produced beautiful silks and cottons in Spitalfields, Manchester and Paisley also grew the best pinks and auriculas, while a writer in 1779 declared that 'scarce a person from the peer to the cottager thinks himself tolerably happy without being possessed of a garden'. The festivals at the beginning of the French Revolution, to a large extent a movement of the artisan classes, invoked nature as the manifestation of goodness and justice. The novels of Jane Austen and the letters of Gilbert White of Selborne in England are a testimony to a world of domestic harmony between nature and design. However, this world rapidly collapsed, as far as design instincts were concerned, into the shadowy cities of desolation and the pretentious and awkward culture they supported, as depicted by Dickens and Zola.

a system of design

When the knack of creating beautiful design was lost in the nineteenth century, many people felt that it must somehow be regained. These reformers sought new and improved rules to replace those shattered in the political and social convulsions of the French Revolution and the Napoleonic wars. They made close links between design and the dominant patterns of scientific thought, which encouraged them to approach the use of nature in design in systematic and analytical ways.

Such an approach was adopted by the German architect and design theorist Gottfried Semper (1803–79), who spent hours in the Jardin des Plantes in Paris in the years between 1826 and 1830. This park housed the Natural History Museum, where Georges Cuvier, one of the great scientists of his day, had organised the classification of species. It was Cuvier's boast that he could reconstruct a lost species from the evidence of a single bone. Semper was aware that evolutionary science could not provide a complete model for the development of architecture. Accordingly, he searched back in time for an explanation of ornament as the outcome of the marriage between function and various processes of making, such as weaving, wickerwork and ceramics. These, he believed, were the origins of human creativity and should return contemporary architecture closer to its origins.

The quest for origins was being carried out in all fields of knowledge. Nature was accepted as the ultimate criterion of truth, but it was also felt that the oldest styles were probably closest to nature – particularly the architecture of ancient Greece, which had only recently been properly recorded. The contemporary fascination with the design of temples such as the Parthenon stemmed from their combination of simplicity and sophistication. The German architectural theorist Carl Bötticher (1806–99) wrote in 1844 that the principles behind the Parthenon were 'completely identical to the principle of creative nature'. This reflected the older idea that nature should not be copied, but understood as a creative principle and abstracted in design. Bötticher's French contemporary, Eugène Emanuel Viollet-le-Duc (1814–79), found the same quality of naturalness in the Gothic style. Both men influenced later generations who at the end of the century created a completely new style based on nature: Art Nouveau.

Owen Jones (1809–74) and Christopher Dresser (1834–1904), two of the most eminent English design theorists of the Victorian age, believed that all historical styles could be analysed and formed into a single system, whose validity would be demonstrated by its natural origins. To remedy their contemporaries' love of natural ornament placed in the most incongruous places, Jones proposed that 'flowers or other natural objects should not be used as ornaments, but conventional representations founded upon them [are] sufficiently suggestive to convey the intended image to the mind, without destroying the unity of the object they are employed to decorate'. Dresser looked for a nature-based style that would be consciously different from previous styles. His plain, unornamented metalware looks 'modern', as though he had successfully anticipated the twentieth century.

Other design theorists rejected the simplification needed for systematic explanations of nature's role in design. Sir Richard Payne Knight (1751–1824) and Sir Uvedale Price (1747–1829), who together developed the theory of the Picturesque, believed that the essence of nature lay in its contradictions and its ability to be more than one thing at a time. In rejecting dogmatism and extreme solutions, their theory of landscape was in tune with the sensibility and politics of the age of Constable and Jane Austen.

John Ruskin, one of the great popular exponents of nature in the next generation, experienced nature in a way that was too complicated to be reduced to any formula. He was not afraid of the complexity of trying to unite nature and design. For him, nature was not so much a source of forms, but a guide to the right way of doing things and a standard of judgement applicable to everything. Ruskin did not want people just to find ornaments in nature, or to admire ancient buildings that achieved a harmony of nature and culture. Nature was a dynamic process of growth and change, from which a variety of practical and moral lessons could be learnt.

Left Iron bursts into leaf in the glazed court of the Oxford Museum (1855–61) designed by architects Deane & Woodward, who were inspired by the ideas of John Ruskin.

The Oxford Museum – the first building for scientific study in that ancient university – was designed by the architects Deane & Woodward, working under Ruskin's inspiration. Completed in 1861 after a slow building process, the museum shows what Ruskin's ideal of a modern building might have been, although he later expressed his disappointment in it. Its external ornament is placed according to Gothic precedent, while its detail was freshly observed from nature by the Irish carvers, the O'Shea Brothers. One of them wrote that he 'would not desire better Sport than putting monkeys cats dogs rabbits and hares, and so on, in different attitudes' to set against the plain surfaces of the exterior. The phrase 'Nature is the Art of God' was due to be carved on one of the museum's walls. However, before the museum was finished, the publication of Charles Darwin's *The Origin of Species* in 1859 undermined Ruskin's simple biblical faith in creation and plunged mid-Victorian thought into a turmoil of religious doubt. The only escape seemed to be an attempt to see everything in terms of evolutionary theory.

Even in the depression caused by his loss of religious faith, Ruskin stood out against materialist explanations of the world and arguments for evolutionary development in art. What Ruskin dreamed of was, in many respects, put into action by the designer, businessman, poet and political thinker William Morris (1834–96). Nature was the touchstone of Morris's activities. His designs for fabrics and wallpapers have a freshness derived from direct observation and careful choice of colours. He has been hailed as a precursor of the ecological movement. In his 1877 lecture, *The Lesser Arts*, Morris made the connection between the design of everyday products and the larger issue of quality of life. He contrasted London before industrialisation with London as it had become: 'We cannot quite imagine it; any more, perhaps, than our forefathers of ancient London, living in the pretty, carefully whitened houses, with the famous church and its huge spire rising above them, — than they, passing about the fair gardens running down to the broad river, could have imagined a whole country or more covered over with hideous hovels, big, middle-sized, and little, which should one day be called London'. Morris's social critique was linked directly to the understanding that a system that destroyed nature must ultimately destroy itself.

Inspired by Morris, the architect and pattern-designer C. F. A. Voysey (1857–1941) created a radically novel style on the basis of nature. He wrote: 'To go to Nature is, of course, to approach the fountain-head, but a literal transcript will not result in good ornament; before a living plant a man must go through an elaborate process of selection and analysis, and think of the balance, repetition, and many other qualities of his design, thereby calling his individual taste into play and adding a human interest to his work. If he does this, although he has gone directly to Nature, his work will not resemble any of his predecessors; he has become an inventor.'

Below The wiry head of an eagle fern (*Pteris aquilina*) illustrates the impression of latent energy in plant stems that inspired Art Nouveau designs.

In his designs, Voysey tried to bring people closer to the goodness of nature through direct and symbolic representation and the avoidance of excessive 'culture'. People who commissioned Voysey houses, like those in the United States who patronised the 'Craftsman' furniture of Gustav Stickley (1857–1946), were in search of what we would now call an 'alternative' lifestyle, rejecting many of the conventions of their class. Some architects tried to sidestep the effects of architectural culture by finding local materials in different parts of Britain, and hoped that the architecture would almost design itself with massive stones, pebbles off the beach or thick thatched roofs.

romanticism in design

In countries such as Hungary and Finland, which had long formed part of larger political units (here the Austrian Empire and Russia), the reassertion of national identity and language at the turn of the nineteenth century was closely linked to the creation of an indigenous style of architecture, expressing peasant culture. This meant going back beyond the international classicism of the early nineteenth century, as seen in the Russian-influenced buildings in the centre of Helsinki, and finding roots in the country. The National Romantic style, practised with local variants by Eliel Saarinen (1873–1950) and Lars Sonck (1870–1956) in Finland, and by Károly Kós (1883–1977) and Odon Lechner (1845–1914) in Hungary, was usually dark and heavy, with rough stone and timbers, suggesting the primitive life of the forests.

The dominant style of the 1890s, Art Nouveau, has already been mentioned as the outcome of much of the nineteenth-century enquiry into plant forms as a source of ornament in place of historical styles. Its exaggerated whiplash curves and melting forms evoked nature's moods of perversity and excess, with shapes that lent themselves particularly well to glass and ironwork. Like Arts and Crafts and National Romanticism, it was a way of supplanting the conventions of academia and developed in parallel with all kinds of utopian social and political projects. Art Nouveau was itself a national romantic style through which new identities were discovered: in Scotland in the work of Charles Rennie Mackintosh (1868–1928), who often based a whole room on the theme of a particular flower or tree; and in Catalonia, where Antonio Gaudí (1852–1926) created buildings that look as if they could be alive and starting to move.

Above 'I do not blame the artist for using only stems, for he has produced curious, unexpected, subtle, amusing and delicate effects from them,' wrote François Jourdain of Hector Guimard's Castel Béranger, Paris, 1897.

In the United States, the Chicago architect Louis Sullivan (1856–1924) observed nature with care and devised intricate patterns for low-relief and stencilled paintwork to ornament his structurally revolutionary skyscrapers. Sullivan's buildings therefore proclaim an apparent paradox: here was a man who liked to say 'form follows function' yet was one of the greatest-ever designers of ornament; someone who believed that a new architecture must include a new decoration 'limitless in organic fluency and plasticity'. Such thinking reflected the writings of the 'transcendentalists', such as Ralph Waldo Emerson and Henry Thoreau, who encouraged a special relationship between nature and the emerging culture of the United States. Sullivan's more famous disciple, Frank Lloyd Wright (1869–1959), proclaimed his close affinity to nature by appropriating the term 'organic architecture' and bringing his long career to a conclusion with the shell-shaped Guggenheim Museum in New York.

The climax of Art Nouveau came around 1900, after which it quickly went out of fashion. It was as if nature had penetrated too far into the realm of culture and upset some invisible balance. Culture reasserted itself, partly through eclectic style revivals and partly through the emergence of an alternative in the strict, formal control and geometry that we recognise under the name of modernism.

modernism, nature and design

What is modernism? It can be understood as the cultural response to the process of social and economic modernisation, or more specifically as a period style from the first part of the twentieth century that addressed these issues in a more or less unified way. In the broader sense, modernism includes a wide variety of responses to nature, some of them in direct contradiction to traditional techniques and forms, others seeking to reaffirm a variety of historical patterns and practices by clearing away the cultural legacy of the Renaissance.

Descartes' philosophical transformation of people into abstractions achieved its fullest expression through the American management thinker, Frederick Winslow Taylor (1856–1915). In *The Principles of Scientific Management* (1910), Taylor advocated the minute study of a worker's daily routine to avoid waste of time and effort, stating: 'In the past the man was first; in the future the system must be first'. In his recent book *Reconstructing Nature*, the English sociologist Peter Dickens argues that the division of labour and knowledge in modern societies 'operates against an adequate understanding of ourselves and our relations to nature'. Charlie Chaplin's fable of revolt against the machine in the film *Modern Times* makes the same point through comedy.

The pioneers of modern design were worried by the adverse effects of industrialisation on the quality of manufactured goods, and on the people who produced them in overcrowded cities. After 1900, instead

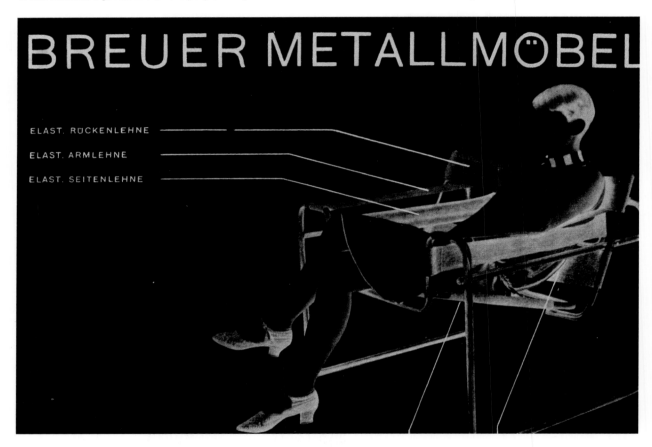

of trying (like William Morris) to establish an alternative world of craft, many began to believe that it was only by collaboration with large-scale industry that the situation could be improved. In 1907 the architect Peter Behrens (1868–1940), until then a leading figure in the Art Nouveau movement, was appointed chief designer to AEG, Germany's giant supplier of electrical equipment and appliances. Behrens wanted to overcome the separation between art and technology, and to design products that would come closer to the true spirit of nature than did the ornamented forms of Art Nouveau. He found virtue in the unselfconscious works of engineers, writing in 1910 that they could be explained as embodying a natural law, the law of mechanical construction: 'It is the law of organic being, which nature also reveals in all her works.' It cannot be coincidence that the Berlin photographer Blossfeldt was taking his hard-edged, machine-like photographs of natural forms at the same time that Behrens was forming his new ideas.

Behrens had three assistants in his office around the year 1910, each of whom was to become famous as a modern architect and designer: Walter Gropius (1883–1969), Ludwig Mies van der Rohe (1886–1968) and Charles-Edouard Jeanneret (1887–1965), better known as Le Corbusier. Each of these

Above Modernism's abstraction of nature into pure geometry is demonstrated by Marcel Breuer's Wassily chair, 1925.

men carried the seeds of modern design in a different direction, but each, in his own way, was concerned with the expression of nature in design. At the same time, nevertheless, they were aware that the conditions of modern industrialised society could not be escaped.

At the Bauhaus, the design school that Gropius established in Weimar, students worshipped nature and practised traditional crafts under the tutorship of the proto New Age master Johannes Itten (1888–1967) in the years immediately after 1919. The ethos changed to become more industrial, but not, Gropius claimed, 'based on an anti-traditional obsession for mechanistic technique qua mechanistic technique ... [which is] doomed to lead to the deification of pure materialism'. In these years after the First World War, the need for a new relationship with nature was keenly felt, and not only in the world of design. The stripping away of ornament, of history and of all kinds of convention created a way of life known as 'Die Neue Sachlichkeit' – the New Objectivity. The profuseness of nature sometimes seemed embarrassing: the Dutch painter Piet Mondrian refused to look at the trees outside his studio window while painting his visions of pure Platonic geometry inside.

More than any other modern architect, Mies van der Rohe worked to present nature in contrast to culture. The extreme simplicity and transparency of his best-known houses, the Tugendhat House at Brno (1930) and the Farnsworth House at Plano, Illinois (1949), serve to draw attention away from the building and out into the landscape. At the Tugendhat House, there is a double wall of glass along one end, with enough space between the layers of glass to grow indoor plants and bring nature even closer.

Of Behrens' three famous pupils, Le Corbusier had the most complex relationship with nature. As a student in Switzerland, he was introduced to the writings of Ruskin and made ornamental designs from pine trees in a National Romantic style. As he matured, he discovered the power of classical architecture, but always responded with extraordinary intensity to places, scenery and planting, giving these priority over any preconceptions about style. He modified his most famous saying, 'A house is a machine for living in', by adding that it was also 'an appropriate place for contemplation', and wherever possible he introduced windows from which nature could be viewed in tranquillity. In the 1930s, he began to doubt the value of machine civilisation and returned to nature and craft techniques of building. Writing to architectural students in 1943, he wanted them to draw from nature: '... this evidence of the organic, these eloquent spokesmen with their size and shape governed by the natural cosmic rules and regulations: pebbles, crystals, plants or the rudiments of plants ... These lessons would replace the dreary study of classical plaster casts that has dulled our appreciation of the Greeks and the Romans.'

As for Gropius, the criticism against which he was trying to defend himself, that modern architecture is divorced from nature and purely utilitarian, is not groundless. The plain unornamented forms of 'The New Architecture', as it was often known, lent themselves easily to factory methods of production; when executed without imagination or care for the lives of their inhabitants, the buildings offered no redeeming features. With products, abandoning ornament did not necessarily result in the beautiful forms that Behrens had designed for electrical kettles or light-bulbs. He specifically warned against 'trying to derive artistic form from utilitarian function and technology'. László Moholy-Nagy (1895–1946), who succeeded Itten at the Bauhaus, was also aware of the danger of an over-mechanical method, writing in 1929 that design should follow 'laws of life which guarantee an organic development'.

Gropius, Mies and Le Corbusier certainly believed that they could use the productive capacity of machines to give people a fuller life in more beautiful surroundings. As far as the planning of cities was concerned, this meant the introduction of more trees and open spaces – 'Sun, space and green' as Le Corbusier expressed it. When Gropius claimed to be following in the steps of William Morris, he was referring to Morris's social ideas and love of nature. Morris, however, did not believe that the industrial system could be tamed or civilised. He and Gropius therefore represent different approaches to the same problem, and produced very different-looking results.

Above The Great Barrier Reef, Queensland, Australia. Made of coral deposits, the reef is the only living structure visible from outer space. It is one of the world's most biologically diverse environments.

The potential reconciliation of craft and industry was demonstrated in the Nordic countries in the 1930s and later. The Finnish architect Alvar Aalto (1898–1976) grew up in the forests and, after experiencing the initial excitement of modernism, wanted to modify its harshness with natural materials and forms. Although not strongly motivated by politics, he shared with other architects of his generation a feeling that an understanding and appreciation of nature was connected to well-being in every sphere of life. He wrote: 'After all, nature is a symbol of freedom. Sometimes nature actually gives rise to and maintains the idea of freedom. If we base our technical plans primarily on nature, we have a chance to ensure that the course of development is once again in a direction in which our everyday work and all its forms will increase freedom rather than decrease it.' Aalto expressed his affinity to nature not only in buildings, but also in his bent plywood furniture and his well-known Savoy vase – a biomorphic form, apparently casually composed, but endlessly fascinating.

dissenting voices

It is possible to describe twentieth-century design largely in terms of a modern style, led by technology and the ideal of progress. However, there have always been voices of dissent, questioning these values and warning against the possible consequences. The counter-movement has taken many forms, from idealistic communities of artists and thinkers to individual craftsmen making things by hand in defiance of industrialism. John Ruskin and William Morris voiced many of these concerns in the nineteenth century, and it could be said that some of their predictions of disaster have come true.

The period after the Second World War established the United States as the world's dominant economic and political culture, with an unprecedented range of consumer goods. However, it gradually became apparent that this pattern of life, which the rest of the world viewed with envy, might not be an unmitigated blessing. Neither the social idealism nor the high aesthetic standards of the European Modern Movement played much part in the American consumer economy, which was largely based on ideas of styling and built-in obsolescence, reinforced by sophisticated advertising. Nature seemed an infinite resource that mankind – having penetrated the mystery of being, by splitting the atom – could exploit to its own ends with ever-increasing sophistication.

From within the design community there was enthusiasm for the revelations and potentialities of science, mixed with a sense of foreboding. In 1951 the design theorist Georgy Kepes, a pre-war associate of Moholy-Nagy, presented an exhibition called 'The New Landscape' at the Massachusetts Institute of Technology, followed by a book of the same name that explored the newly revealed structure of matter. Nothing was presented at its actual scale. The enlargements of crystallography were juxtaposed with aerial photographs of landscapes. Kepes wrote: 'Science is only one component of the understanding that we need for a well-balanced attainment of human ends. In our chaotic and direction-less world, it gives us two-edged weapons – powerful tools and ideas with which we may either create or destroy.'

Destruction, shrouded in secrecy and defended by the economic power of big business, became increasingly evident through the 1960s as the American counter-culture began to see the connections between the materially comfortable lifestyle of the individual, and the damage that could be done all over the world. This was a destruction not just of nature, but also of human relationships. Increase in car ownership and use began to have adverse consequences on patterns of city living, while the dependence on chemicals for increasing agricultural production became another source of concern. From 1960 onwards, criticisms of environmental damage like Rachel Carson's *Silent Spring*, were matched by criticisms of urban renewal such as Jane Jacobs' *The Death and Life of Great American Cities*.

It seems undeniable that one of the greatest changes in the history of ideas in the whole of the twentieth century will prove to be the spread of ecological or 'green' awareness during the 1960s and 1970s. At first, government and big business denied both their responsibility and the likelihood of disaster, but after two or three decades of readjustment, opposition to green ideas is no longer a viable political position. What, then, are the consequences for design as a practice, and for ordinary people's engagement with it?

The pattern set by the Industrial Revolution, driven by the need to produce more goods and develop more markets, may be coming to an end. In western countries, levels of consumption are no longer the principal indicators of standard of living, and the idea of quality – in personal possessions and surroundings, in opportunities for work and leisure – has

Below The crystals of cholesteryl acetate, seen through high magnification, display the extraordinary beauty found in the structure of matter.

become increasingly important. Consumers are learning to resist buying products that they believe to be unethical, and are recognising a responsibility not only to themselves and their families but also to wider social groups and other societies.

To link these issues to design is to give design a much larger role than it normally assumes. There was a time in the 1980s when design seemed to have become a self-referential game for a privileged few, ignored by most of the world. The ethical ambitions of modernism in design were temporarily discredited, but they have re-emerged through post-modernism's greater flexibility of design language, which can be interpreted and shared like a joke between designer and consumer. The message-carrying capacity of design has been re-invigorated, sometimes with irony, but often also with a genuine desire to communicate ideas directly, and through technical developments that change society without producing objects as such. The Internet, for example, was inspired by the ideals of freedom and sharing that developed in the 1960s. The concept of recycling is having an increasing impact on design, but has no tangible or visible form. At the same time, the look, touch and feel of designed objects remains an important aspect of their potential to create change.

With the opening in 1997 of the Guggenheim Museum, Bilbao, by Frank Gehry (1929–), a growing architectural trend towards organic form suddenly became highly visible. There is hardly a straight line in the whole structure, which glitters in its titanium carapace. Whether it is supposed to be animal or vegetable, it gives the feeling of a living organism. In his book *The Architecture of the Jumping Universe* (1995) the American theorist Charles Jencks identified the forms made by Gehry, Daniel Libeskind and others as the architectural equivalent of 'new science', with its post-Newtonian view of the universe, implying the end of simple relationships of cause and effect. Jencks claimed the results as 'the return to a different nature'. If Newton was one of the pillars of the mechanistic world view that Jencks believes has constrained architecture until very recently, then Descartes was the other. There is an equivalent shift towards a post-Cartesian architecture based on intuition, sensuality, human relationships and a deeper understanding of nature.

The abstract, mathematical understanding of nature as a design source, which was dominant earlier in the twentieth century and underlies modernism's relationship to nature, has been modified by a more multivalent response to the whole phenomenon of nature. The contemporary English architect Christopher Day writes: 'All senses have their parts to play – in ugliness or in beauty – but all too often they are considered in isolation. When together, giving the same message, they start to speak of the underlying essence of a place. When sensory messages conflict, environmental improvements are just playing with cosmetics. Just as Concorde may look like a beautiful bird but doesn't sound like one, a beautiful well-landscaped façade fronting a heavy main road is a nonsense.'

The contemporary Anglo-American architect and theorist Christopher Alexander has worked for many years to find ways of explaining why one thing is more beautiful than another, without referring to culturally constructed standards of beauty. He speaks of objects, even quite simple ones, as being 'a picture of the self', meaning that people recognise something in themselves that corresponds to the quality in the object. Every aspect of the thing contributes to this sense of it being alive – its colour and material, but most particularly the way the appearance of the whole is built up as a composite to achieve unity in diversity; a rich experience rather than an example of 'impoverished reality'. In Alexander's system, ornament becomes not only legitimate but also essential. Nature is the ultimate source for ornament, but not by literal transcription or copying past styles. To achieve the living quality, it is not necessary that a thing should be made by hand, although an individual maker is most likely to find it.

Alexander's method produces buildings, such as houses in Mexico and California and a college at Eishin near Tokyo, that are strikingly similar in character to the Arts and Crafts architecture of around 1900. This demonstrates that the attempt to follow nature at that period was an unfinished project waiting to be taken up again.

Hand making is one way in which to search for beauty. The effect is not just on the look of the product, but also on the whole being of the person doing the making. In his essay 'Are the crafts an anachronism?', the English theorist Brian Keeble describes how, while serving material needs, the maker 'keeps the inner eye of spiritual vision on those things that relate to his final end – the fact that he is a created and creative part of that sacred reality that is the world. By so doing he produces an environment that forms the living context for the human spirit to participate in the cyclic rhythms of nature that are themselves a reflection of the cosmic rhythms of nature.'

Left The Villa Uunila, Finland, is built in traditional ways, partly from salvaged materials, and with attention to the conservation of energy. Designed as a homage to the Finnish architect Alvar Aalto, its wooden pillars suggest forest trees, against a background of wave-form panels.

One of the most interesting symptoms of economic change in the last twenty years has been the emergence of a younger generation of skilled craftspeople, ranging from creative artists to conservators and repairers, who have deliberately chosen a way of life that many people thought to be doomed. In industry, steps are being taken to reverse the damaging effects of the division of labour and to give workers a greater sense of personal involvement in the work of a company.

The effect of ecological thinking, taken to its ultimate conclusion, may be the redefinition of design as a comprehensive awareness of relationships between things and people. This would be in line with changes in scientific thinking that stress the importance of process in nature, rather than the study of the finished object. The American writer Paul Hawken believes that 'we have a thousand years of work ahead of us – brilliant, sustaining, innovative work, a profound act of citizenship and participation that harmonises the relationship between commerce and nature'.

This harmonisation could go far beyond limiting damage to the physical world. The future of design opens up long-forgotten possibilities of human insight into our own place in the world. Merging the long-separated realms of science and the humanities, and dissolving the modern anxiety of alienation from the world and from each other, it can allow us pleasures which do not cost the earth.

The idea that nature is 'designed', is a plausible assumption in the face of the evidence. Patterns of all kinds reveal themselves to the eye, some on the surfaces of animal skins, leaves or tree bark, others in the geometric arrangements of seed heads, snowflakes, the spirals of a shell or the movements of the planets and stars in the sky. Still deeper versions of these patterns can be seen with the microscope. The diversity of inspiration from nature is astonishing, and designers have always borrowed from these structures in the course of solving problems or just gratifying their own sense of order.

Nature offers instances of ingenious technology, particularly in the way that plants disperse their seeds. The burrs that stick to clothes in search of some new site for propagation were the inspiration for

design in nature

Velcro. Similarly, seedpods gave the Austrian design theorist Victor Papanek (1925–98) the idea for a series of pods for individual doses of medicine. There are a few more examples of such specific borrowings, but the greater part of natural inspiration in design is visual rather than mechanical.

What is the reason for nature's richness of pattern? Is it all a function of adaptation to environment and of the struggle to survive? What pattern-forming mechanisms underlie the structure of matter to bring about results in which the pattern features of one species or material are so similar to another? These questions have begun to receive answers in recent years. The results have the capacity to alter many of our assumptions, bringing back to nature many of the associations of beauty and wisdom that were traditionally found there, and which have important implications in cultural, even political terms.

Previous page The emerging spiral form of this succulent shows the principles of growth found in many plants and shells.
Right A storm in the Bering Sea seen from Nimbus 5 satellite. The largest and smallest forms in nature reveal the process of growth and change.

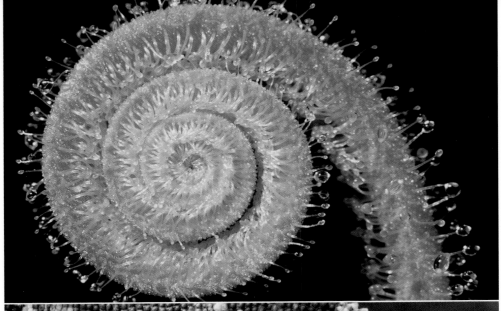

Left The coiled leaf of the thread-leaf sundew and the chameleon's coiled tail show the practical application of good design principles in nature.

The ecological movement has created a justifiable anxiety about mankind's relationship to nature. It has urged us to pay more attention to the lessons of the natural world, for the order of nature is not just visual. It includes the cycles of birth, life and death, the cycle of day and night, and the cycle of the seasons. Nature is not just about objects; it is also about systems and the shifting relationship between an object and its context. It has much to do with submission to the cycle. This is ancient wisdom, but it has taken a long time to re-learn it through the medium of modern science.

order and change before science

Most cultures have creation myths. The creation of the world in seven days, as described in the Bible, has a magnificent mythic completeness. Even though few people now wish to take it literally, it is hard not to imagine some outside agency of creation to which the beauty of nature can be attributed. That life came about entirely by chance coincidence, as neo-Darwininists claim, seems unlikely. The counter-claim of the contemporary American biologist Stuart Kauffmann that life is a quality inherent in pre-biological matter, and could be expected to generate itself spontaneously in a number of situations, seems more plausible. Such a scenario requires no mastermind, no blind watchmaker, to be present at the moment of creation.

Above Man and the earth are placed at the centre of traditional cosmology, as shown in the illustration by Gregorius Reisch to the Margarita Philosophica, 1535.

When the ancient Greeks looked into the structure of the universe, they were searching for broad principles rather than specifics. Some of the most powerful Greek writing deals with the unpredictable and cruel power and wonder of nature. The opposite view was presented in the writings of Plato (427–347 BC), who saw the world as an ordered series of geometric structures of pure form, created by a mastermind. The five 'Platonic solids' corresponded to what were then seen as the elements from which the universe was made. Thus, the Cube corresponds to the Earth, the Octahedron to Air, the Pyramid to Fire, the Icosahedron to Water; while the Dodecahedron sums up all the elements as the Cosmos. This schema represented an unchanging structure underlying the apparent disorder, with a strong theological implication that mankind was raised above the rest of creation and given the intuitive ability to understand it. Aristotle (384–322 BC), in his book *Physics* (the Greek word for 'Nature'), reconciled Plato's stable structure with the earlier idea of flux, showing how change was in fact part of the structure of the world. 'Surely nature longs for opposites and effects her harmony from them,' he said. 'The structure of the universe – I mean, of the heavens and the earth and the whole world – was arranged by one harmony, through the blending of the most opposite principles.'

Another tradition of thought stemmed from the Roman philosopher Plotinus (204–70 BC), who in his writings, the *Enneads*, made a synthesis of Christianity, Plato, Aristotle and earlier Greek philosophy. Plotinus was not concerned to expose the mechanisms of nature, but rather to communicate the way in which nature is a window through which the soul of the individual can regard the great universal soul. He makes Nature say: 'The mathematicians from their vision draw their figures, but I draw nothing: I gaze and the figures of the material world take being as if they fell from my contemplation.' This is an expression of the inscrutable quality of nature that is understood not through analysis but through the sympathetic link which we feel with nature, while still being separate from it.

Plotinus's vision shows man in harmony with nature, drawing a wordless inspiration from it that has no practical application, but which would undoubtedly influence the making of any work of art through the ideal of beauty and harmony. Lucretius (*c*.99–55 BC), the poet follower of the philosopher Epicurus in Rome a century before Plotinus, saw life as continually changing; humans are like relay runners, passing on its torch. Physical science taught them that the only things that exist are atoms and empty space. There is no life after death, gods play no part in the governance of the world, and the pursuit of pleasure is the only rational goal. Epicurean philosophy is at odds with mainstream western thought, with its assumption that design in the universe implies a rigid mathematical order. Yet Lucretius's world of whizzing atoms, powered by their own desire to generate, has many echoes in modern scientific and social thinking.

That the universe is a rational construct is one of the essential presumptions of western thought, fundamental to the way that law and government are justified as being part of the natural order. This is probably the reason why modern science originated in the West, when the idea of law was translated back from its metaphorical application to nature to the realm of human affairs, and was taken as a literal concept for describing nature – as in the 'laws' of physics or biology, which can validate the way non-scientific decisions are made. Joseph Needham, the great historian of Chinese science, explains that the situation in the East was very different, because of the fear of political tyranny: 'The old conceptions of natural law in the form of accepted customs and good mores proved more suitable than any others for Chinese society in its typical form.' The idea of natural law arose from the fact that all beings were part of 'a cosmic or organic pattern', and what they obeyed were the internal dictates of their own natures.

Deductions about our place in the universe, made from the design of nature, have had an immense impact on human behaviour. The original dispute among the ancient Greeks about the relative importance of order and chaos has usually been resolved in favour of order, since we tend to fear the unpredictable outcomes of disorder. But an excessive respect for order is self-defeating, since it restricts the possibility of growth, as recent science has demonstrated. Part of the general lesson of nature is to understand the way order and chaos are interrelated.

Above The spiral growth of ammonites is typical of many shells. Brilliant colours are created during fossilisation by mineral crystallisation.

shapes and structures

Looking at a diversity of objects in nature, we see certain common patterns and proportional relationships that are signs of order. The proportion known as the Golden Section is encountered in many natural forms. It involves dividing a line into two parts so that the relationship between the small and large parts is the same as the relationship of the larger part to the whole. There is only one point at which this can be done, but the system can then be multiplied up indefinitely. Hence, in many natural forms, such as the skeletons of horses and frogs, a series of related Golden Section proportions can be found. These Golden Relationships occur, for example, between different leg bones, the spine, neck and skull. The Golden Section can also be presented in the form of a spiral that coils outwards according to a hidden pattern of squares and rectangles. Most spiral forms of plants and shells conform to some variant of this pattern.

Of the 'designed' qualities of nature, the Golden Section is one that has been used – whether consciously or not – in the design of objects as varied as ancient Greek pots and the basketry hats of American Indian tribes. Its proportional relationships also underlie the harmony of music, and it is normally seen as a natural proof of beauty. The Golden Section proportion is an irrational number – that is to say, one that can only be expressed with an infinite series of recurring fractions at the end. The Fibonacci sequence, discovered by the thirteenth-century Italian mathematician, Leonardo da Pisa, is an approximation to the Golden Section in terms of whole numbers. Each number in the sequence is the sum of the two preceding ones: 0, 1, 1, 2, 3, 5, 8, 13, 21, 34, etc.

This is the basis of phyllotaxis, the ascending spiral arrangement of foliar and floral organs, a subject which has fascinated designers investigating the natural world. In sunflower seed heads, for example, the spiral lines that the eye picks up are 'logarithmic' spirals that are more tightly curled at the centre and extend out, flattening as they go. These lines appear to be longer in one direction, and the ratio between the number of spirals in each direction is that of consecutive numbers in the Fibonacci series. The numbers themselves may vary between different species of sunflower, but they are always numbers from the Fibonacci series.

The Fibonacci series does not derive just from evolutionary or environmental causes but also from a basic manifestation of natural structure. It is not so much the number of the seeds that is significant as the constant angle between them. In 1837 it was discovered that this is an angle of 137.5 degrees, which allows for the maximum efficiency of packing. In fact, irrational numbers turn out to provide the best conditions for packing, so the widespread occurrence of the Golden Section is not so surprising.

The packing structure of protein molecules supplies the determining geometric structure of the DNA double helix chain, which was discovered by James Watson and Francis Crick in 1953. This was one of the major scientific revolutions of the century. As a visual form, however, the double helix was known long before its discovery as a scientific structure, and it can be found at a larger scale in natural and man-made objects. One striking example of this form is the Renaissance double staircase at Pozzo di San Patrizio, Orvieto, Italy, by Antonio da Sangallo the Younger (1483–1546).

The human body has provided one of the principal guides to proportion and design for many centuries. Many of its 'designed' characteristics, such as its bilateral symmetry, are shared with other animals, but it also provides a series of measuring devices, such as the inch (the length of a thumb), the foot, the fathom (the width between outstretched arms) and the cubit (the length of the forearm). These have emerged spontaneously among different cultures. The metric system lacks this direct relationship to the body, and dispenses with the numerical sequences (often featuring subdivisions of twelve), which allow for more whole-number fractions. The human body, particularly the face, also exerts a considerable subconscious influence on our sense of

Below The head of a daisy (Leucanthemum vulgare) shows the spiral arrangement whose numerical relationships are those of the Fibonacci series.

rightness and appropriateness in design, leading us to seek balance and centrality, with not too much visual weight at the very top or bottom.

The number system in traditional civilisations is much more than a means of calculating quantities. It is a realm of symbolism which connects the visible proportions of the physical world to an invisible mental structure. Each of the numbers up to twelve has many layers of meaning. For example, three variously represents three-dimensional space; time, considered as a beginning, middle and end; and numerous religious systems, including the Holy Trinity. The number seven is traditionally connected with the cycles of human life (such as the days of the week and the Seven Ages of Man) and the stars (for instance, the Plough).

The architect Le Corbusier became interested in reviving proportional

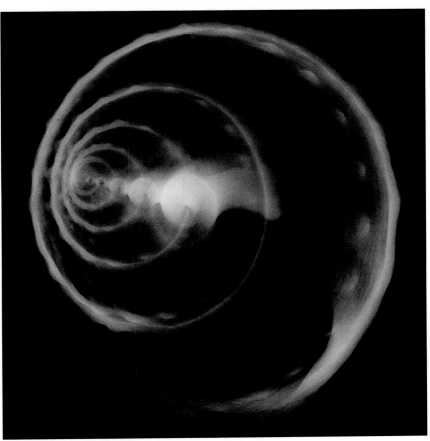

Above An X-ray photograph of the inner chambers of a marine snail shell reveals a 'logarithmic' helical spiral. This incremental curve has been described as 'a pyramid coiled round a vertical axis'.

systems for a metric age as a way of restoring human scale in architecture and design. He called his system Le Modulor (a combination of 'module' and *or*, referring to gold). It was a return to the stream of tradition that flowed through the Renaissance from the ancient world and is equally embodied in classical and medieval architecture, but stripped down to its abstract essentials.

colour, texture and pattern

While the pattern of the Golden Section can describe many of the structures in nature, it does not describe what it feels like to look at nature. Much of the attention the artist or designer gives nature is focussed on the effects of shape and form. Animal skins and feather patterns are among the most striking and individual examples that have been copied in design, or even transferred – as actual skins and hides – into the making of things. High levels of contrast in colour and tone are among the features that make these natural forms specially valuable as design sources. Patterns in leaves and flowers may also be contrived by a garden designer or reproduced in textiles or other media. With these examples, the designer may wish to lure the eye by producing an underlying variety within an overall uniformity.

The underlying causes for such patterns in nature are varied, and may include camouflage, sexual attraction and the signalling of danger. Like the omnipresent Golden Section, patterns such as that of a giraffe hide, which so closely resembles the cracking patterns on the surface of dried mud, may have a common origin in the tendency of lines of stress to make three-way junctions. In these cases, the design 'function' of these lines in nature is probably only incidental to the decorative value of the effect.

Crystalline patterns are among the most fascinating and complex in nature, and include such clearly visible phenomena as snowflakes, with their repeated branchings at 60 and 120 degrees. Crystals, in the form of rocks, can display their structure on a massive scale in the landscape, or more intimately in cut gemstones, carrying us into a pure world of abstract geometry.

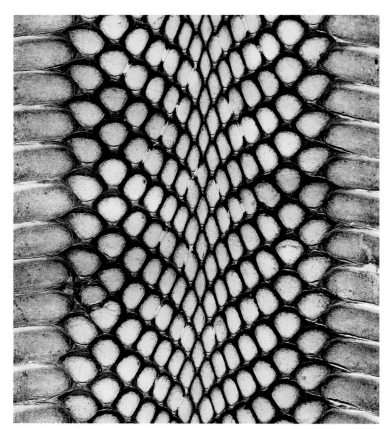

Above A cobra skin shows the patterning caused by tension, which creates a honeycomb effect as lines appear at the weakest points.

In all these kinds of pattern, the fascination for the human eye is in the alternation of what is called 'figure' and 'ground'. The eye selects a figure as a pattern out of a mass of visual information, leaving what is not the figure to be seen as ground. The distinction of figure and ground seems to be deeply inherent both to our way of seeing and to nature's way of constructing visual language. The ability to read and understand the world according to figure and ground patterns is, some theorists claim, the basis of verbal language as well.

While some aspects of natural structure can be adapted as three-dimensional engineering, much of nature provides an impulse for decoration that is essentially two-dimensional. It is particularly characteristic of nature to make the figure–ground relationship ambiguous – there is no single 'correct' way of reading it. We may variously see the single unit of a leaf, the negative space beside it, or the emerging pattern of leaves, all similar but different, and each with their negative space. Although in some instances there may be a functional reason for this, it must remain for the most part one of the unexplained but most emotionally powerful design aspects of nature. Such ambiguities can also provide the most satisfying, life-like qualities in a man-made pattern.

In the act of transformation into design, some of the disorder of nature is replaced by human order. However, some of the most successful nature-based patterns successfully abstract the natural form, while retaining a liveliness of overall design that we recognise as being the essence of nature. Turkish carpets are a good example, as are many other so-called primitive forms of design, such as Polynesian bark-cloths and African pottery. Flat pattern designs based on leaves and flowers have been a feature of Chinese, Japanese, Middle Eastern and western cultures, with some striking similarities between them. Some of them look abstract, but their roots can nonetheless be related to natural forms.

Through the study of nature-based artefacts of all ages, and by reference to nature itself, we can reach an understanding of the designed quality of nature that goes deeper than functional evolution, genetics, microbiology or adaptive behaviour. There is a strong feeling that this is how we are supposed to look at the world, if only because it is so deeply satisfying. Seeing nature as a shifting pattern of figure and ground brings us close to the contemplative experience of the mystics. Without needing to deny anything that science has taught us, it simply brings additional meaning to the whole.

a deeper meaning

The idea that nature opens up access not only to individual forms but also to a whole new understanding of form has always fascinated designers. The English-born engineer Ove Arup (1895–1988) spoke in 1952 about the possible meaning of 'organic' in terms of concrete shell: 'One may find approaches to it in nature – in the structure of a leaf, a sea-shell, a soap-bubble – although I would not suggest that nature is always economy-minded. But one feels intuitively that if one had infinite knowledge of structure, and if one could put the material where it was wanted, our structures might take a very different shape. They might be more complicated, with folds, ribs, etc., like the cabbage leaf, or they might take the form of shells of subtle shape with varying thickness and reinforcement distributed in fine strands wherever needed, although the idea of reinforcement may be wrong in itself. In simple cases, one can almost feel what the logical or "organic" structure would be.'

In engineering, nature teaches the value of lightness. The French engineer Robert Le Ricolais (1894–1997) expressed the art of making an efficient structure as 'adequately distributing the maximum number of holes'. He was particularly interested in radiolarii, the tiny sea creatures that fascinated Darwin, and wrote: 'You can't just convert these things into building structures, but there is much to admire and understand. You see some kind of coherence and a purity of design which is amazing, which is frightening.'

Frank Lloyd Wright found inspiration in a wide range of natural forms in different parts of the USA. He described the saguaro cactus as 'a perfect example of reinforced building construction ... a truer skyscraper than our functioneers have yet built'. In most cacti, he found that nature employs continuous tubular construction with considerable structural economy. Reflecting on the desert camp that he built in Arizona in 1929, the precursor of Taliesin West, Wright felt that 'we pay too slight attention to making slight buildings beautiful or beautiful buildings slight'.

Of all the great figures of modern architecture, the Finnish architect Alvar Aalto showed in the most inventive and varied ways how the design of buildings could relate to nature. His architecture, closely rooted in his country of lakes and forests, was influenced by the rationalised technical and social architecture of modernism in the 1920s. However, he also saw how modernism in the 1920s was incomplete because it soon became a formal language like classicism, rather than being motivated by the desire to create a new relationship between man and nature in human society. His work appeals on

Below The timber wolf is well disguised in the snowy forest, not only by its colour but also in terms of the ambiguity of figure and ground between the animal and its habitat.

a popular level to people who find much modern architecture too chilling and intellectual. Aalto's buildings, such as Viipuri City Library and Säynätsalo Town Hall, engage the physical senses through their textures and materials, while his use of light and space has a quality, found in nature, of unfolding complexity resulting in overall unity.

holism and the new science of nature

The concept of holism is the opposite of the Cartesian belief that the truth about things is best discovered by breaking them down into smaller subsections. Holism requires that everything should be seen as part of its context, as the sum of figure and ground, because if the context is altered, any living thing will also change, as will our perception of it. Although each part may contain elements of truth, it is only in the totality that the 'real' truth can be found. This is an experience familiar to the artist or the designer, who is usually practised in the skill of focussing in and out of a picture or design to see alternately the parts and the whole, and to imagine the possible effect of certain changes. It is another layer of meaning in the discussion of 'design in nature', which reveals a different kind of 'design' to any considered so far.

As an account of how the eye and mind can 'see' in this special way, we have John Ruskin's description of a country walk in France: '... getting into a cart-road among some young trees, where there was nothing to see but the blue sky through thin branches ... the branches against the blue sky began to interest me, motionless as the branches of a tree of Jesse on a painted window ... Languidly, but not idly, I began to draw it, and as I drew, the languor passed away: the beautiful lines insisted on being traced – without weariness. More and more beautiful they became, as each rose out of the rest, and took its place in the air. With wonder increasing every instant, I saw that they "composed" themselves, by finer laws than any known of men. At last, every tree was there, and everything that I had thought about trees, nowhere.'

This kind of intuitive 'seeing' constitutes an alternative to the normal analytical consciousness. Designers solving specific problems often move between the two modes of consciousness, since it is often through lateral thinking, or by holding the problem in a mind engaged on something quite different, that the most beautiful and most original solutions will emerge. Holistic or non-analytical consciousness is a subordinate mode in the everyday world, but since nature conceals much of its truth from purely rational analysis, it is worth considering as a necessary way of engaging with nature, whether the purpose is scientific inquiry, visual inspiration or pure pleasure.

In the same way that figure and ground interact in nature, so we ourselves can interact with nature instead of treating it as something external to ourselves. This is not easy to describe briefly, but is a capability inherent in the human mind which theorists believe is lost only through conditioning in another system. Our habitual analytical consciousness persuades us that there is something behind the phenomena that we see: some world of ideal forms, or a set of mechanisms, including those currently favoured as total explanations: genetics and evolution.

Holistic consciousness is against reliance on the unseen or metaphysical. It can be described by the cumbersome term 'phenomenological', which insists that the phenomena of nature, if seen properly, contain in themselves everything we need to know about them. Among the important aspects of this movement, which has grown in importance since the beginning of the twentieth century, is the potential it offers for the unification of arts and sciences by favouring subjectivity and intuition, and its critique of the dangers of over-rationalised science in working against nature. An awareness of the problems of rationalism, and the potential of its alternatives, has been particularly strong in German science and philosophy. It stretches back to the time of the poet and scientist Wolfgang von Goethe (1749–1832), and thence to the founders of Gestalt psychology, which aimed for unity in the study of the mind, and the appearance of a science of ecology, dealing with the unity of the earth. Much of the scientific development of the last hundred years has involved the dismantling of the universe of Newtonian certainty and its replacement by a holistic alternative. Nils Bohr (1885–1962), Albert Einstein (1875–1955) and Werner Heisenberg (1901–76) shifted conceptual understanding of the physical universe with the theories of relativity and quantum physics. The dualism of order and chaos that the ancient Greeks had grasped began to reappear from the ruins of the lost order, with new ways of understanding disorder and appreciating its creative potential.

Above Florets of Romanesco broccoli are 'self-similar' at all scales: an example of of fractal geometry.
Left The saguaro cactus made Frank Lloyd Wright dream of a perfect skyscraper.

The early stages of this revolution in understanding nature happened alongside some of the most exciting activities in the visual arts in the century, in the Weimar Republic in Germany in the 1920s. There, as the Austro-American scientist Fritjof Capra writes, 'the entire culture ... saw itself as a protest movement against the increasing fragmentation and alienation of human nature'. The most exciting developments have happened in the last thirty years, as the new mathematics of complexity has exposed the impossibility of properly describing nature in the terminology of rationalist science.

The 'Gaia hypothesis' of James Lovelock and Lynn Margulis brought together for publication in 1972 a great deal of revolutionary scientific thinking that looked at change and flow, rather than fixity, in nuclear physics, biology and chemistry. Lovelock realised that it was the instability in the earth's atmosphere, controlled by systems such as feedback loops, that sustained life and prevented it from disappearing into the entropy, or slowing-down, that conventional science would predict.

This insight was equivalent to holistic ideas: seeing that individual parts are all working within a larger whole. It also carried an ecological lesson, that damage in one place can upset overall balance. The Gaia hypothesis does not necessarily imply that the world is designed, still less that there is a designer 'behind it', but it does allow nature to be mindful and intelligent.

The sciences of the mind have come to play an important part in this regeneration of knowledge. The Chilean neuroscientist Humberto Maturana established the concept of autopoesis, the pattern of organisation of living systems, in 1974. This was one of several research exercises that came close to showing how order emerges out of chaos by setting up regular cycles and loops, and how nature depends on self-generating and self-perpetuating mechanisms that link up into larger networks. It is possible to extrapolate from the biology of cell structures to show how autopoesis can be a model for understanding the relationship of parts to a larger whole, even in social structures.

Among the limitations of older scientific methods was the tendency to ignore small variations and deviations and to round things into whole numbers. Quantum physics began to create doubt about the view of hard, solid particles of matter arranged in linear systems, and the development of computers made it possible to look at these small differences as manifestations of a dynamic web of interrelated events. The word 'chaos' is used in contemporary science to describe this greater level of complexity, rather than complete randomness. In *The Fractal Geometry of Nature* (1984) the French scientist Benoît Mandelbrot revealed some of the visual complexity of natural forms discovered through the computer. Fractals have no particular application in design, but they do reinforce the intuitive belief in the wholeness of nature, a belief often defended by artists and designers against the evidence of science.

truth and beauty

Nature is the traditional standard of 'truth and beauty', but these absolute values have become suspect in a world that accepts no ultimate standards and tends to see everything as relative. Now that changes in science are altering our view of the world, it will be interesting to see whether truth and beauty will return with their relevance reinforced.

Designers are the people who have the privilege of shaping the images of a better future that everyone carries in their head. It is hard to imagine a restoration of beauty and truth without an accompanying understanding of people's material and spiritual needs and a desire for greater social justice than the world has ever seen. This inevitably places politics at the centre of the design issue, as many designers have always insisted, although many others have also treated people as abstractions and worked within a confined world of peer-group approval, rather than for society as a whole.

If, as many think, those in the developed countries will soon have to undergo massive changes to their lifestyle in order to achieve sustainability, it is necessary to show how this future can be better than the industrialised present, with its consumer culture of aspiration and restless striving. It is possible to imagine that, in a simpler regime, truth and beauty derived from nature will seem meaningful once more.

The Austrian artist and teacher Rudolf Steiner (1861–1925) made a connection between politics and forms created in the spirit of nature. He proposed a schema of world epochs, predicting an epoch of aesthetic pleasure, which Steiner believed would occur around the beginning of the third millennium (that is, about now), when 'the mental abilities of a man who is intellectual and at the same time immoral will definitely deteriorate'. After that would follow an epoch when 'cleverness without morality will be non-existent'. This may sound like a pious wish, but Steiner characteristically linked it to the power of art and design, learning from nature, to achieve the process of transformation: 'Buildings will begin to speak. They will speak a language of which people have as yet not even an inkling.' This startling prediction involves design in its widest meaning – as the whole way in which we, as the global population, decide to organise our lives.

Left The Waterside offices for British Airways at Heathrow, by the Norwegian architect Niels Torp, 1998, are not only economical in energy use but are also designed to reflect a concern for the happiness and effectiveness of the people working there.

41

design in nature

When designing the chapel at Ronchamp, in the Vosges area of France, in 1950, Le Corbusier picked up a crab shell on Long Island and kept it by his drawing board. It is easy to see how it may have inspired him to choose a roof form unlike anything he had ever designed before, curving up at the sides like a shell, which has natural strength and rigidity in its thin, brittle material. Designed as it was by an arch-modernist, Ronchamp changed the course of architecture. Its sculptural, three-dimensional quality inspired architects to move from the Cartesian grid-like structures of early modernism and to seek inspiration from nature. Le Corbusier's contemporary, the German architect Eric Mendelsohn (1887–1953), was another architect in love with shells. On his desk he kept a nautilus

shells and skeletons

shell, one of the most impressive natural spiral forms, and with this inspiration to hand, devised many beautiful spiral staircases (such as that in the De la Warr Pavilion at Bexhill-on-Sea, Sussex). Mendelsohn wrote of this 'marriage of our productive idea with the organic creative power of nature'.

During the same period, Frank Lloyd Wright in the United States was declaring that the only proper architecture was 'Organic architecture – the architecture of Democracy', an architecture 'of Nature, for Nature', which avoided the symmetries of classicism. Wright's great exposition of the spiral was the Solomon R. Guggenheim Museum in New York, which uses the form inside and out. It is no coincidence that when the Guggenheim recently built another museum in the Spanish city of Bilbao, the American architect Frank Gehry created one of the most imaginative organic architectural forms of the twentieth century. He was helped by the most advanced computer technology to leave almost no flat plane or straight line.

Previous page
The shell forms of Renzo Piano's Tjibaou Cultural Centre, New Guinea, are a striking adaptation of natural forms in contemporary architecture.
Right Le Corbusier reverted to natural forms in his late buildings, nowhere more so than in the Chapel of Notre Dame du Haut at Ronchamp, France, 1955.

structure in architecture

Architects have looked to nature for inspiration from the earliest times. The column capitals of ancient Egypt were based on lotus leaves. The architects of classical Greece formalised other aspects of nature into their column capitals. Sometimes they did this beyond conjecture, as with the acanthus leaves of the Corinthian capital. Sometimes the process was subtler, as with the diminishing spirals of the Ionic capital, which may be based on rams' horns or the shell form. Writing in the first century BC, the Roman architect Vitruvius looked back – as many have done since – to try to imagine what the first buildings might have been like, and assumed that they would have been inspired by sources in nature such as the nests of swallows. Somewhere along the line, as he had to explain, things became less obviously based on nature, but the need to work with nature in all sorts of ways remained central to his definition of good architecture. Nature provides the materials, imposes the conditions of the site and, on another level, determines the formation of human society for which the buildings are created.

There has never been one single form of relationship between architectural structure and nature, but rather a series of overlapping ways of using nature as a standard and an inspiration. Particular ornamental forms can be easily identified with plants and animals; others, like the Ionic capital, are generic natural forms in which the geometric structure of nature has been abstracted. As for the engineering aspect of building, there are plentiful analogies between skeletons and built structures, and between shells and the curved, rigid surfaces of many buildings. Indeed, the skeleton and the shell define two basic types of structure (although by no means the whole range: load-bearing walls, for example, have no counterpart in organic nature, their closest resemblance being to the rock strata from which stone itself is quarried). It is often difficult to say whether a building form derives directly from a natural source or simply resembles it by accident. Judging from pottery and other artefacts, mankind's desire to use natural forms seems to have emerged through a process of generalising and stylising.

Just as nature makes a separation between skeleton and soft tissue, the same separation of structure and cladding occurs in many types of architecture. Most plants reveal a distinction between their principal load-bearing structure and the more flexible and expendable part – as a tree does with its trunk, branches and leaves – while designers seldom want their buildings to display parts that are disproportionate or useless.

engineering from nature

Although buildings, unlike objects in nature, generally have to stay the same shape once they are completed, plenty of architects have managed to suggest that their buildings are actually growing like plants or animals. This dynamic quality in architecture belongs to no single period or place. It seems to come into existence at times when designers listen attentively to the language of nature as a whole. The kind of architecture we call Baroque, current in the seventeenth and eighteenth centuries, derived its name from an Italian word for a misshapen shell. Baroque designers expressed the disorderly quality of nature, its surging and heaving masses, particularly those associated with rocks, caves and oceans. Francesco Borromini's steeple for the church of St Ivo in Rome spirals up to the skyline like an encrusted shell. Gianlorenzo Bernini's fountains in Rome, which depend on the movement of water in sunlight to complement and animate the stone sculpture, embody the essence of the style.

Below The volutes of the Ionic column are said to be derived from curls of hair, or perhaps from the horns of sacrificial animals such as rams.

Above The spiral lantern of Borromini's church of St Ivo della Sapienzia (1662) bursts up like a growing form amidst the rooftops of Rome.

The rational minds of the seventeenth century began to find this degree of emotion excessive. Following Plato's belief that nature has an inherent order, they wanted to get beyond the flesh and return to the skeleton as the hidden structure of the universe. It remained a matter of conviction that the ancients of the classical world had based their design system on nature, as the evidence of their architecture and the surviving texts proved. The modern age therefore felt itself justified in using its superior knowledge to improve on the past. For some historians, this self-conscious moment around the beginning of the eighteenth century defines the beginning of modern architectural thought. The mythology of classical architecture was stripped away and replaced by a scientific outlook that ran in parallel with the investigation of nature. Claude Perrault (1613–88), the amateur architect at the court of Louis XIV who did much to achieve this change of direction, even died of an infection caught as a result of dissecting a camel for research purposes. These investigators, with their minds set partly on the engineering possibilities of building, discovered that the despised Gothic style, even more than the classical, was a system in which the load-bearing skeletal structure was clearly expressed.

Although structural engineering may appear to be a sober problem-solving activity, it has its own romantic side. Large-scale engineering structures, such as aircraft hangars, are impressive in their scale and lightness of structure. The great halls of international exhibitions aimed to impress as well as provide uninterrupted space for exhibits. It was a gardener, Joseph Paxton (1801–65), who, as a member of the committee charged with choosing a building for the Great Exhibition of 1851 in Hyde Park, applied his experience of glass and iron greenhouse structures to the problem of building a cheap temporary exhibition hall. It was thus that he came up with the concept for the Crystal Palace. His expertise in designing these structures owed less to existing architectural knowledge than to his achievement at Chatsworth (where he worked for the Duke of Devonshire) in nurturing and sheltering a giant South American lily, called the Victoria Regia in honour of the sovereign. The Lily House, which has sadly been demolished, was based on the combination of rib and gutter found in the lily itself, and the same system was later transferred to the much larger Crystal Palace. Similarly, the American engineer and inventor Buckminster Fuller (1895–1983) found one of the most appropriate uses for his lightweight 'geodesic' domes in the US Pavilion at the Montreal Expo of 1967, which still stands.

Unlike architectural design, engineering is a rational problem-solving process which looks to nature for solutions, and is often free of the pressure to conform to precedent required by society and culture. Thus, although the structures designed by engineers may not be beautiful as a matter of course, they can be among the most striking and astonishing, apparently sharing nature's laws of economy and integrity, where each element works towards a particular purpose. The bridges and grain elevators created, often by unknown engineers, in the same years as the heavily decorated buildings of the late nineteenth century stimulated the revolt against historic styles and the beginnings of modernism. It was like wandering out of an over-cultivated garden full of hybrid plants into a meadow or forest where everything could be seen more clearly for what it actually was.

using new materials

New materials were well suited to the possibilities of refined structure. As Bessemer converters made steel cheap and readily available in the 1860s, it replaced iron as the principal structural material. Steel girder bridges, where all the structural members are exposed, look very much like skeletons, although in design terms they act quite differently. Reinforced concrete, a material that was developed in France in the late nineteenth century, was highly suitable for exploring an architecture of ribs and bones. It can stretch and bend in all directions, the chief constraint on its use being the cost of building the timber formwork into which it is poured. A new age of bridge building began, with thin lattices of riveted girders that could carry ever-longer spans. The bridges of Robert Maillart (1872–1940) in rural Switzerland, built in the 1920s, have always had a strong appeal because of their instinctive 'rightness', achieved entirely within the constraints of engineering form and often in settings of great natural beauty.

As was discovered in the 1930s, concrete can also be made into shell forms – thin membranes curving in space, held rigid by their own curvature like a curled piece of paper. Sculptural forms in shell concrete were particularly popular in the 1950s, when the techniques were still quite novel, and labour was relatively cheap in Europe compared to the cost of materials. From the sports stadia in Italy by Pier Luigi Nervi (1891–1979) to the TWA terminal at Kennedy Airport by Eero Saarinen (1910–61), the expressive qualities of concrete were a fulfilment of modern architecture's promise to return to the sources of nature. It was also evident, however, that this approach to nature was best suited to the creation of large spaces under a single roof. Since then, economy has demanded the substitution of other materials for large roof spans. Nevertheless, the Mexican engineer Felix Candela (1910–97) continued building in this way, with a highly skilled pre-industrial workforce, who carried buckets of concrete by hand up wooden scaffolding and worked with the minimum amount of timber formwork. More recently, Santiago Calatrava (1951–), a Spanish engineer highly regarded among architects, has continued the tradition of expressive structure, preferring skeletal forms for the design of transport interchanges and bridges in the grand manner of the nineteenth-century engineers.

While Candela could float a shell of concrete as if it were a handkerchief falling through space, the German engineer Frei Otto (1925–) pioneered the use of cable-net and textile coverings in tension as a way of roofing large spaces. Among the best-known of these structures are the German Pavilion at Expo 67 and the Olympic Stadium in Munich (1972). Otto's inspiration comes from geometry and physics, rather than directly from nature, but since he is dealing with the same engineering problems that plants and animals have to confront, his work tends to resemble natural forms, obeying the same physical laws

Right The 'Geodesic Dome' built in 1960 at the Climatron Botanical Gardens, Missouri. Designed by the American inventor and environmental campaigner R. Buckminster Fuller, it is one of over 300,000 such structures to be built all over the world.

Above The tensile cable-net roofs of Frei Otto's Olympic Stadium, Munich, 1972, show the practical application of forms that are in tune with the forms of nature.

and achieving analogies with landscape, molecular form and reptiles. Candela and Otto belonged to a generation of designers who welcomed all the help that nature could give to their design concepts.

materials from the earth

Steel and concrete are materials derived from nature at a distance, requiring industrial processing from raw materials. They can be used in juxtaposition with nature to great effect, by contrasting with their background or imitating natural effects. However, the symbolic meaning of nature can also be displayed through raw materials, and for some people this gives a greater satisfaction.

Stone has enjoyed a revival in recent years; some architects have found an almost Ruskinian quality of 'aliveness' in it. Some of the most commonly used building stones, such as limestone and marble, are sedimentary, composed of the shells of living creatures laid down under water and raised above sea level by changes in the earth's crust. Architects can select 'beds' of stone from the quarry which display shells and fossils openly, as did Alison and Peter Smithson (1928–93;1923–) with the 'Roach bed' Portland stone of the Economist Plaza in London in the 1960s. Other stones can bring a quality of strangeness, beauty and ancient times into a contemporary project, like the narrow strips of slate that form the inner walls of contemporary Swiss architect Peter Zumthor's recent Thermal Baths at Vals in Switzerland.

Timber shares the same high-tensile strength of steel and reinforced concrete. It is also warm to the touch and brings, in its grain, its own pattern and texture. It has many cultural meanings, often suggesting the forest from which it came, or the symbolic trees that link earth and heaven. The classical architectural orders of western Europe originated in simple timber post and beam construction, possibly with some mystical meaning. The symbolic architecture of Buddhism is also based on timber prototypes, translated into stone and depicting the structure of the universe in an ascending hierarchy of distinct elements. In Japan, the simplest wooden temple architecture belongs to the indigenous Shinto religion – a religion that incorporates animistic beliefs revering spirits in nature – rather than to Buddhism.

In Hungary under communism in the 1970s and 1980s, Imre Makovecz staged a kind of one-man protest against the regime by retreating to the forests and building timber structures in defiance of the centralised building laws, which demanded the use of industrial techniques. These buildings illustrate aspects of Hungarian folklore and language (the latter since many of the words for parts of buildings are the same as words for parts of the body) and continue in a specially localised way the symbolic meanings found in timber buildings everywhere.

the greening of architecture

The great architects and engineers who rediscovered the organic possibilities within modern architecture were concerned with economy, efficiency and beauty. To their concerns, our own age has added a new anxiety about nature, which has grown up through the ecological movement.

There are several ways of defining a 'green' or ecological building whose overall intention is to create the minimum damage to the environment. Energy consumption in use is one of the most important, which means that artificial heating and cooling should be employed as little as possible. By making the best use of natural methods of heating and cooling, by exploiting the cycle of the seasons and all hours of the day, it is possible to manage without air conditioning and with greatly reduced heating, even in extreme climates. This is known as Passive Solar Architecture. Methods for channelling air naturally through the building can be learnt from traditional structures in hot countries. The narrow, crooked streets of Arab souks were designed to provide shade and to keep the air in motion, making a more comfortable walking environment than a wide boulevard under blazing sun. In northern climates, the sun's energy can be gathered by solar panels and converted into electricity to supplement heating.

Architects can minimise environmental impact through their choice of materials. Some materials, notably steel and glass, consume a great deal of energy in their production. Recycling materials can give access to timber, brick and slate from demolished structures – which may also be very attractive visually. As with most building materials, however, there is an environmental cost in transportation. An ideal building material would be found near the site and would be a renewable organic resource (such as the coppice timber that was harvested from trees in traditional forestry), an abundant mineral resource (such as building earth) or a resource that can be reused in more than one building (which allows the use of stones and bricks in soft mortar). Waste products, such as straw bales, are also attracting attention for their potential in building, while fast-growing plants like hemp are being introduced for the first time.

Learning from local building traditions and adopting local materials are valuable ways of ensuring that a building fits into its surroundings. Adaptation to environment does not require that a building imitate natural forms literally, as some of the more extreme examples of green architecture have attempted to do. It requires an intelligent and sympathetic dialogue with a particular place, such as traditional buildings seem often to have achieved.

It is almost impossible to build without making an environmental impact, and the search for the best solution involves a mixture of the most sophisticated and the most simple technologies. Many different kinds of building claim to be 'ecological', including skyscrapers in the developing cities of the Far East, but these claims are debatable, since the buildings usually employ high-energy, non-renewable materials and are 'green' mainly in their avoidance of the worst excesses of energy consumption in use.

The Eden Centre in Cornwall, by Nicholas Grimshaw and Partners, is an interesting example of high-tech design adapting itself to nature. Under construction in 1999, the building consists of a curving glass roof covering an old china clay pit, forming an artificial environment for growing tropical plants – effectively a huge greenhouse. The design is curved to fit the contours of the clay pit and will reproduce four different climatic zones, including a 60m-high rainforest canopy. Instead of a conventional glass and steel structure, the 'biomes' (as the greenhouses are called) will have an exoskeleton of lightweight steel. From this will be hung an envelope of EFTE foil, a transparent film, formed into a three-layer pneumatic pillow and inflated under low pressure by small electric motors. The energy needs of this system will be met by photovoltaic cells. Thus, it is hoped, the biomes themselves will function, live and breathe using their own form of photosynthesis.

There is a continuing discussion about the true definition of 'green architecture'. It can be treated principally as a technical matter, but many architects believe that it requires a commitment to improving the social function of buildings, not least so that they should achieve their maximum potential and avoid obsolescence. The architect Trevor Garnham explains the need for architecture to find 'appropriate and eloquent forms to reshape the built world in relation to the natural world', and thereby to go beyond merely technical answers. The new British Airways headquarters by the architect Niels Torp is a good example of many new office buildings where not only is energy being saved but a pleasant, less formal working environment is also encouraging creativity.

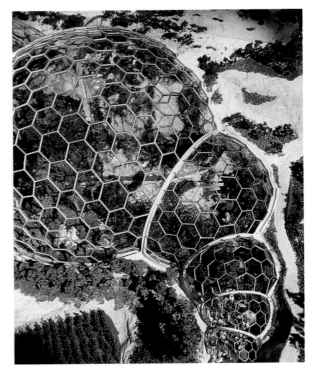

Below The Eden Centre, Cornwall, has the fantastical quality of the 'stately pleasure-dome' imagined by S. T. Coleridge in the poem Kubla Khan.

Above The catenary curves
of a spider's web.
Right Brooklyn Bridge, New
York, by J. A. and W. A.
Roebling, 1869–83.

Nature provides engineers with models that are both aesthetic and practical. The catenary curve of a spider's web, the shape automatically taken up by a chain or string when not pulled tight, is a simple and satisfying form that suggests the line of least resistance. It forms the basis of the suspension bridge principle, as beautifully displayed in Brooklyn Bridge. The use of twisted wire rope cable here creates a lighter kind of suspension bridge in which physics and aesthetics combine to form a parallel to nature. Le Corbusier called the bridge 'full of native sap'. More rigid bridge structures look like skeletons, although freedom of movement is not part of the design brief. Bones depend on the additional strengthening of muscles, which hold the structure together and provide the means for its movement, while bridges like South Grand Island are constructed from a series of boxes and parallelograms. Like bone, steel has some strength when bent, but is more reliable in compression.

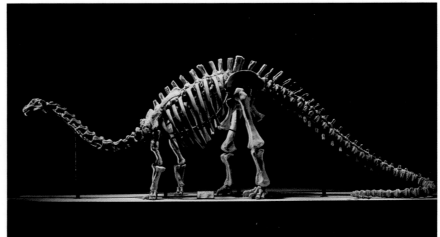

Top South Grand Island
Bridge, New York.
Above Skeleton of a brontosaurus.

The idea of rib structure has analogies with bones and with trees. Contemporary architects have returned to the design of rib structures in timber for the range of expressive qualities they can achieve. The effect can be as light and soaring as a grove of young trees, as in Fay Jones's chapel; or dark and enclosing, like the inside of a whale, as in Imre Makovecz's windowless mortuary chapel in Budapest. In the field of precast concrete structures, Santiago Calatrava has revived the excitement of an earlier age of engineering, with a strong sense of the underlying order of nature, its proportions, scale and symmetry. The radial ribs of the main roof covering the air–rail interchange of Lyon Station suggest, without direct imitation, the thinness and curving geometry of fish bones.

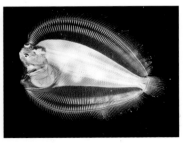

Opposite Mildred Cooper Chapel, Bella Vista, Arkansas, designed by Fay Jones, 1988.
Top La Grande Gare de Satolas, Lyon, by Santiago Calatrava, 1992.
Above Delicate curving bones on a flat fish.
Left Farkasrét Mortuary Chapel, Budapest, by Imre Makovecz, 1975.

Houses often 'grow' out of the landscape by virtue of their shapes and materials, especially when the stone is not even quarried, but found lying in the fields.

A different kind of growing appearance is achieved by resemblance to animal or vegetable form, as with the Pineapple at Dunmore, Scotland, or the Prairie House in Oklahoma. Alternatively, buildings may borrow from the qualities of nature, as in the Whiting House in Sun Valley, which reflects the curves of hills behind it. The use of an open form, planned without a strong grid and allowing for changes and additions, enables a house to be a growing thing, in contrast to a neat and finished box. Buildings such as the Empie House in Arizona, which appears to grow out of the rocks it stands on, require a freedom to be unconventional, and are most often found standing isolated in wild tracts of country.

Above The Whiting House in Sun Valley, Idaho, by Bart Prince, 1992, follows the shape of the hills behind.
Right Charles Johnson's Empie House at Carefree, Arizona, 1982, designed to achieve a unity between building and landscape.

shells and skeletons

Far left Herb Greene's
Prairie House at Norman,
Oklahoma, 1962, has been
compared to a wounded
buffalo, but the architect
was in fact thinking of a
mother hen, giving shelter
and security.
Left The Pineapple,
Dunmore, Stirling, Scotland,
built in 1761–77 to overlook
a kitchen garden.

shells and skeletons

Above The gradually unwinding helix of a gastropod shell, cut away to show its geometric form. **Right and above right** Eva Jiricna's pirouetting staircase for a house in Rutland Gate, London. **Opposite** Frank Lloyd Wright's Guggenheim Museum, New York, 1943–59.

The spiral of a shell form lends itself to the design of staircases, whose geometry resolves into a pattern when looking down from the top. In traditional spiral staircases the treads are cantilevered from the surrounding wall, but when the staircase can stand alone in space – as do Eva Jiricna's shining constructions of steel and glass – the effect is even more striking. The result is an astonishing pirouette in space. While Jiricna's staircases resemble the twisted strands of the DNA double helix, Frank Lloyd Wright's controversial design of the Guggenheim Museum in New York is more like the truncated section of an actual shell, since it grows wider as it spirals upwards. Wright loved the spiral form, and would have used it more often had it been better adapted to the practical purposes of buildings. While Renaissance architects used it for ramps up which horses could be ridden, the commonest modern application is for multi-storey car parks.

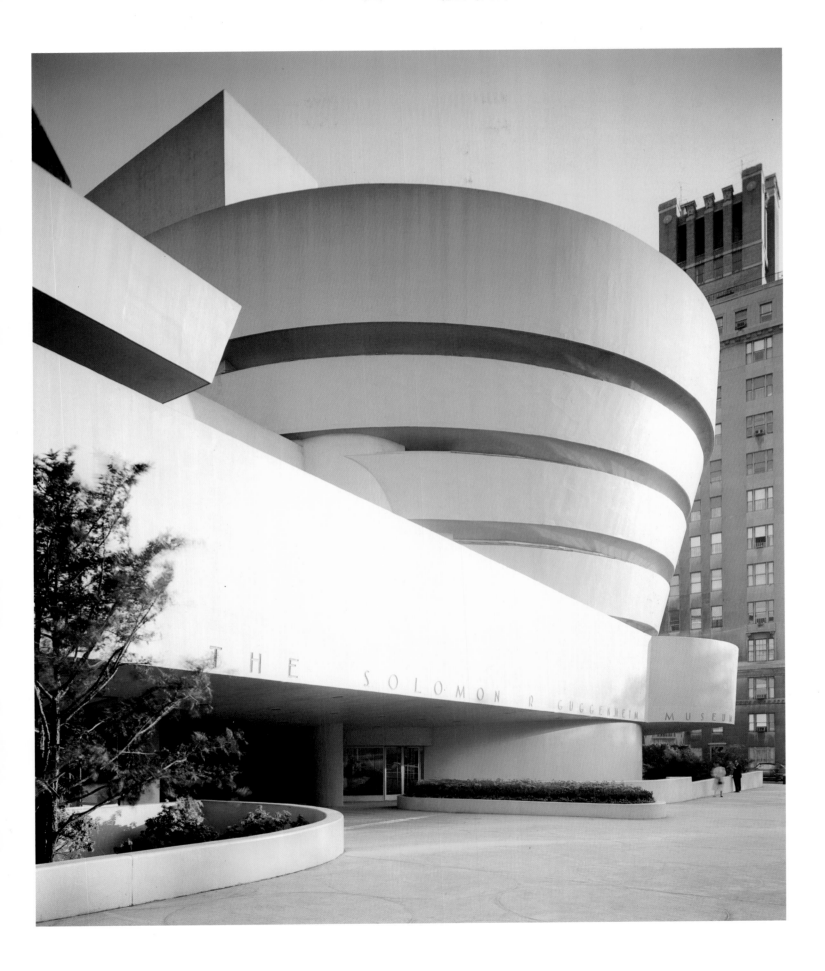

shells and skeletons |

Clockwise from top A root form with architectural potential; the wind-eroded Wave Rock at Hyden, Australia, suggesting concrete forms in building; TWA Terminal, Kennedy Airport, New York, by Eero Saarinen, 1956–62; Truss Wall House, Tokyo, by Ushida Findlay, 1993; staircase of Steven Holl's Museum of Contemporary Art, Helsinki, 1997.

Straight lines are seldom found in organic nature.
In architecture, too, curves have their uses, adding
strength to thin walls and roofs. Curves can also
achieve beautiful effects, which enhance the three-
dimensional intensity of the space and provide surfaces
for modulated light, as in Steve Holl's staircase for the
Museum of Contemporary Art in Helsinki.
Before computers, the calculations required for building
curved forms such as Eero Saarinen's terminal at
Kennedy Airport were formidable; they also went
against the rationalistic spirit of the 1950s. But in
trying to capture in concrete the experience of flying,
Saarinen created a building that now seems far ahead
of its time in displaying so strong an interest in the
expressive potential of organic form. In the same vein,
Ushida Findlay's house in Tokyo is an abstract exercise
in the fluidity and connective properties of the
construction system known as the truss wall.

The idea of living rock has always inspired awe in the designer, and buildings often recreate the effect of rock strata. The fourteenth-century chapel of St Govan in Pembrokeshire – one of the most geologically varied parts of Britain – was built from the same stone that forms the cliffs behind it. Charles Johnson's Empie House in Arizona encloses boulders that are 570 million years old, in a structure which simply roofs over the spaces between the rocks with giant log beams. Contemporary architects are becoming increasingly interested in the expressive power of stone. Peter Zumthor's Thermal Baths in Switzerland feature layers of stone descending evocatively into water. This building shows how modern architecture and the ancient tradition of finding health in water have been brought together to create an extraordinary experience. The Swiss architects Herzog & de Meuron, working at the Dominus Winery in California, have used rubble held in wire to create contrast between an ordered grid and the accidental variation of individual stones found in a traditional dry stone wall.

shells and skeletons |

Clockwise from top
St Govan's Chapel, Pembrokeshire, Wales, fourteenth century; a graphic display of rock strata in Capital Reef National Park, Utah, USA; Dominus Winery, Napa Valley, California, USA, by Herzog & de Meuron, 1997; Thermal Baths, Vals, Switzerland, 1997; Empie House, Carefree, Arizona, USA, by Charles Johnson,1982.

Above and right Villa Mairea, Finland, 1937–39, was built by Alvar Aalto in typical Finnish woodland.

At the Villa Mairea, Finland, Alvar Aalto designed according to his belief that the influence of nature was needed to humanise modern architecture and make it a true means of bringing beauty and freedom to everyone. The forest surrounding the villa inspired the multitude of timber columns, grouped together in different formations, which support the staircase as it descends into the main living room. The result is almost like a little woodland enclosure. Live plants add to the effect, and the view of nature continues through the large window beyond. Aalto's father was a forester and he learnt how to apply technology respectfully to nature. He wrote: 'The most striking of standardisation committees is nature itself ... [generating] a richness of form that is inexhaustible and moreover in accordance with a given system.'

Right Westminster Lodge, Hooke Park, Dorset, by Edward Cullinan Architects, 1995.
Below The Temple of Time, Oshima, Japan, by architects Benson and Forsyth, 1993.

What is ecological architecture? It encompasses the organic forms of Edward Cullinan's Westminster Lodge, ingeniously built from woodland thinnings (which are normally discarded), as a lesson on the marriage of high and low technology. Benson & Forsyth's Temple of Time takes a more symbolic view, since it is not a habitable structure. It contrasts traditional technology, found in one half of the building, with the rationalist present, represented by concrete. Each has its part to play in climatic conditioning. Engelen Moore's design, meanwhile, looks like the most up-to-date form of modern architecture, paying no special heed to the ecological credentials of its materials. However, it is designed with an understanding of airflow for cooling, a method which is gradually being rediscovered as a sustainable alternative to air conditioning. Turf roofs, too, although they may be too 'green' for some people, provide excellent insulation in winter and prevent overheating in summer.

Above The Ruzzene/
Leon House, Sydney,
1997, by architects
Engelen Moore.
Left A turf roof nestles in
the landscape at the Post
Ranch Inn, Big Sur,
California, USA.

Right Bart Prince makes
wood do strange things in
a house at Corona del Mar,
USA, 1991.
Below Antonio Gaudí's Casa
Batlló, Barcelona ,1904–6.

Left The armadillo
(*Dasypodidae* family),
a creature with evident
architectural potential.
Below Sydney Opera House
by Jørn Utzon, 1956–66.

Buildings which depart from the straight path often achieve similarities to nature that may not even have been consciously intended. Roughness of external texture tends to recall the appearance of creatures such as the armadillo, and Antonio Gaudí's buildings, like Casa Batlló in Barcelona, are a tribute to the variety of form and texture that the architect found in nature. The curved surfaces of the Sydney Opera House and the Guggenheim Museum, Bilbao, are based more on geometric calculation than on specific sources in nature, but both benefit from a protective plate-like shell much like a crab's. Their families of related forms make them instantly recognisable.

Explorations into new materials for construction, such as tensile fabric, also have their natural corollaries. The roof of the Imagination building, braced like sails with solid masts and spars, recalls the skin stretched over the extended skeleton of the bat's wing.

Above Detail of the Imagination building, London, with its teflon-coated PVC roof designed by Ron Herron, 1990.
Left A brown bat (*Myotis lucifugus lucifugus*) with outstretched wings.
Right The Guggenheim Museum, Bilbao by Frank Gehry, 1997.

67

shells and skeletons |

'To dwell is human,' said Ivan Illich in his address to the Royal Institute of British Architects in 1984. 'To dwell is an art. Every spider is born with a compulsion to weave a web particular to its kind. Spiders, like all animals, are programmed by their genes. The human is the only animal who is an artist, and the art of dwelling is part of the art of living.' The American architect Charles Moore (1925–93) wrote that dwelling 'is not, especially in the tumultuous present, an easy act, as is attested by the uninhabited and uninhabitable no-places in cities everywhere'. Nature can contribute in many ways to remedying this problem of the modern world. It has a special place in the shaping of homes, where the psychology and beliefs of the occupiers play an important part in evolving social habits and design forms. A house is

nests and habitats

somewhere set apart from nature in order to keep its destructive and dangerous forces, whether of climate or predatory creatures, at a distance. It is connected to nature by its setting, its materials and its constructional method, as well as by more subtle forms of symbolism. In this way, the quality of life for the individual and for society can be affected by the design of homes, which have always had the potential to add to our subconscious understanding of who we are.

images of the home

Houses in fiction, particularly in children's books, provide a more vivid impression of the nature of 'houseness'. Where the characters are in the form of animals, as in the English children's story *The Wind in the Willows*, the houses assume even more the character of nests, with all the psychological security that this implies. It is probably not a coincidence that the classics of children's literature in the English language, including the works of Beatrix Potter and A. A. Milne, coincided with the rise of the Arts and Crafts movement in the 1880s and 1890s, which rediscovered the virtues of being at home with nature. In Sweden, the artist Carl Larsson (1853–1919) was creating an ideal old-fashioned family house in the country at Sundborn, which he made famous through his books and illustrations. His book *At Home*, published in Sweden in 1899, became popular through a German edition of 1909 called *The House in the Sun*. These houses all looked backed to the past in certain ways, but nature rather than history was their standard of truth in searching for archetypal images of home.

Recognising the instinctive rightness of images of home in children's books, we can begin to see that houses which we normally treat as more or less pleasant and convenient have an underlying dimension of symbolism, relating them to ancient beliefs about mankind's place in the world.

In primitive societies, it was impossible not to imitate nature in the building of houses. Every action was understood in a symbolic as well as a practical sense, as we can still see in the nomadic tent, or yurt, with its central smoke hole representing the axis between Earth and Heaven. The Earth is symbolic of the Great Mother in many

Previous page The Wall-Less House by Japanese architect Shigeru Ban, 1998, dematerialises architectural structure. **Below** Wightwick Manor near Wolverhampton, originally built for an industrialist, is a Victorian revival of the Elizabethan manor house.

cultures, while the sky is the realm of a male god. There is frequently a triple association between the house, the human body and the Cosmos. In many traditions the gods were born in caves, literally from the Earth, and cave temples are found in many places, notably in India, where the living rock is carved with great elaboration.

Houses such as those of the Batammaliba people in Togo and the Republic of Benin show a detailed level of analogy between the house and the body. Part of a continuous cycle of social ritual, they correspond to an elaborate coded system of reference to men and women. Although the houses do not actually look like people, they are felt to be so alive that you can use them as a drinking companion; one elder at a funeral told an anthropologist: 'I wanted to drink with someone and no one was around, so I used the wall to keep me company.' In many modern cultures a similar sense of respect is attached to the principal hearth and fireplace.

The exact placing of a house in the landscape is also an important matter. Although it is uncommon today for architects to relate to the site of an intended house other than through a visual analysis, many people sense the instinctive 'rightness' of the siting of traditional houses. The siting of churches towards the east is one surviving element of a much more extensive body of practice that responds to invisible lines of energy in the Earth. The ancient science of geomancy existed to formalise these relationships between mankind and the Cosmos in the process of building. A section of the contemporary architectural avant-garde is resurrecting similar practices. The fascinating island park of Hombroich near Düsseldorf, with buildings by leading contemporary minimalist architects like Tadao Ando and Claudio Silvestrin, includes a 'geomantically designed house of clay' by Dietmar Hoffmann.

Above The oculus, or eye, of the Pantheon in Rome remains open to the sky, and suggests the dome of heaven with the sun at its zenith.

nature and domesticity

The idea of designing houses suitable for living in harmony with nature has recurred with increasing frequency. In the second half of the nineteenth century, middle-class houses began to lose their association with nature as cities expanded. However, there existed such a strong feeling about the value of nature to health that a determined effort was made to reaffirm the link between houses and nature, often through reinterpretations of medieval and Tudor styles. In the English style of the 1870s called Queen Anne, even an idealised early eighteenth century became part of the association of nostalgic nationalism, focused on an idealisation of nature. In reconstructing the image of 'home', symbols of security and inwardness – such as steep roofs, small windows and big fireplaces – were emphasised.

This association defined the new aspirational style, which was developed further by architects of the Arts and Crafts movement such as C. F. A. Voysey. It seemed as if the discontents that moved William Morris to advocate revolutionary socialism in the 1880s could in reality be solved by front gardens with hedges and green-painted wooden gates, or perhaps in the more dreamlike, imaginative creations of Charles Rennie Mackintosh. The rusticity was not necessarily false, but when commodified as the suburban semi-detached house of the twentieth century, the idyll became less idyllic.

For a contemporary equivalent to the strong idealism of Voysey and Mackintosh, we might look today to the self-build movement founded in the 1970s in south London by the Swiss émigré architect Walter Segal (1907–85). Segal enjoyed the English tradition of closeness to nature and felt that more people could share it if they built simple timber houses for themselves. His designs for these were practical and lightweight, not imitating nature as such, but getting in its way as little as possible.

Through books and magazines, English houses of the late nineteenth century captured the imagination of Europe. Early garden cities offered a new social vision of modern life and were built by German industrialists before the First World War as an alternative to over-crowded tenement blocks. In the United States, suburbs sprang up under free enterprise development around the great cities, including architectural masterpieces of individual house design by Frank Lloyd Wright in Chicago and Greene & Greene in Pasadena. The quietly luxurious Villa Mairea in a woodland setting in Finland, built in 1938 by Alvar Aalto for the Gullichsen family, was a turning point in his personal rediscovery of nature. A famous photograph of the single-storey house at Kevinge near Stockholm by Swedish architect Sven Markelius (1889–1972), buried in beechwood and with the architect's naked children enjoying the garden, became an emblem of Swedish social democracy after the war. The contemporary Swedish landscape architect Thorbjörn Andersson writes: 'The photograph testifies to an inherited Swedish view of nature, in which people are at home in the wild and live in an intimate relationship with the natural world.' In Stockholm, the same freedom was given to all city dwellers through a network of parks and open spaces.

Architecturally, suburbs were predominantly derivative of historic styles. Although castigated equally by urban renewal theorists and ecologists alike, they doubtless contain a powerful message about people's desire to live with nature, trees, open skies and quiet.

materials from nature

The principal material selected for building a house is dependent on local conditions and cultural traditions, but nature is often interpreted through the adaptation of building materials in houses. Mud is a primal material that has survived in some cultures, including in the West. It tends to be considered as culturally 'backward', but it has considerable ecological value as well as pleasing tactile and visual qualities. In addition, it costs virtually nothing if available on site.

The Egyptian architect Hassan Fathy (1900–89) is a hero to the many architects today who are worried about the wholesale importation of unsuitable western technology in developing countries. Fathy rebelled against this effect of modernisation in his country in the 1950s and revived the age-old practice of building with mud, observing, experimenting and employing a few old craftsmen who still knew how it was done. Fathy wrote: 'Surely it was an odd situation that every peasant in Egypt with so much as an acre of land to his name had a house, while landowners with a hundred acres or more could not afford one. But the peasant built his house out of mud, or mud bricks, which he dug out of the ground and dried in the sun. And here, in every hovel and tumble-down hut in Egypt, was the answer to my problem. Here, for centuries, the peasant had been wisely and quietly exploiting the obvious building material while we, with our modern school-learned ideas, never dreamed of using such a ludicrous substance as mud for so serious a creation as a house.'

Even in the highly regulated and industrialised building culture of Britain, a few pioneers have established precedents for obtaining permission for new earth buildings, some traditional in architectural form, some more artistically innovative. An alternative way of using earth in building is to make a turf roof or bank earth around the building, making what is known as an earth-sheltered building. This is a good way of giving thermal insulation and disguising the building in the landscape.

The versatility of timber makes it one of nature's finest building materials, well suited in size to domestic use. The English tradition of timber framing is based on the dimensions and strength of the oak tree. The posts, beams and curved braces seen in the great medieval barns are like an indoor forest. The design of the traditional timber frame included a range of hierarchical distinctions within the timber itself, distinguishing the best-sawn faces of the wood from the less good. These were used to emphasise the principal spaces in the hall – the main room of every house. In Malaysia, there is a traditional rule of 'one house, one tree'. The nine major house posts must be cut from a single tree trunk and then

positioned so that they reproduce their original relationship when they were one piece. The Japanese tradition of timber building shows its sensitivity to nature not only in construction but also in a response to surroundings. As the editor of *Studio* magazine, C. G. Holme, wrote in 1936: 'We have much to learn from the tradition of Japan where nature comes first: and the architect does not set out to dominate or destroy the surroundings of the house, but to render homage to them. The delight and sympathy with nature entails a kind of camouflage.'

water and bathing

Water is a natural element usually found in connection with gardens, whether in a simple garden pond, or in a tank, pool or basin out of doors. As with flowers, water can seem licentious and wasteful in the wrong places, but its potential for soothing and improving the atmosphere has hardly begun to be appreciated, let alone included in house design as a normal feature. Bathrooms are going through some interesting changes, however. No longer just the minimal hygienic tiled spaces of the past, they are becoming rooms for austere pleasure, without superfluous decoration, but with an almost religious atmosphere. Nevertheless, Christianity, unlike other religions and cultures, does not have rituals for bathing and has historically tended to treat the body as sinful.

The only European countries that treat bathing as more than a way of washing are the Nordic ones from which the sauna originates, chiefly Finland. There, the sauna is felt to be a necessity, shared by all classes of society and all ages, but the individual sauna pavilions built for summer homes by Finland's many lakes can have a special beauty as architecture. Alvar Aalto built several, which are among his most attractive and timeless buildings. Here the bather can enjoy nature as an essential part of the experience, recalling traditions of mud bathing and other outdoor communions with nature.

Water is soothing to look at in a house, and the beautiful and simple houses of Luis Barragán (1902–88) in Mexico found new ways of using the traditional enclosed pool, enhanced by the brightness of the light and the architect's colour schemes. In India and the Middle East, the use of fountains, rills and basins, both indoors and in courtyards, acknowledges the value of moving water in hot climates, and continues as a living tradition. Frank Lloyd Wright's most famous house, Falling Water, was built in the wilds of Pennsylvania overhanging a waterfall; the result is one of the most intensely romantic images of a house close to nature. Wright's admirers range from the American Bruce Goff (1904–82) in Oklahoma, author of wildly fantastical designs, to the cool abstraction of the first work by Norman Foster (1935–) and Richard Rogers (1933–): in 1964, as part of Team 4, Foster and Rogers designed Creek Vean, a Wright-influenced house on the slope of a river creek in Cornwall, which included an early example of a turf roof.

Left The pleasures of water in the open air, experienced in a hot thermal mud tub at the Beppu Spa, Kyushu, Japan.

gardens and domestic landscapes

Gardens can be practical, providing fruit and vegetables or preserving privacy, but they are also symbolic, whether people are conscious of it or not. More than houses, gardens represent an interchange between nature and culture, where some of the dangers and disadvantages of wild nature can be ignored. This demonstrates the paradox that *natura naturans*, unaltered nature, requires a frame of culture before its qualities can be fully appreciated. On a practical level, even the simplest garden cannot be created without a sense of personal collaboration with nature, which is both humbling and instructive.

We tend to think that our admiration for the beauty of flowers is spontaneous, but it seems, like many such things, to depend on cultural conditioning. The Greeks and Romans used flowers as an important part of their religious iconography. In Rome, for example, although water was scarce in the cities, potted plants of fennel, lettuce or barley were grown by mourning women to mark the festival of Adonis and the rebirth of spring. Egypt, with its equable climate, provided a source of cut flowers for the whole Mediterranean, especially for the making of garlands, and aromatic plants were also highly valued.

Although the enjoyment of images of flowers was widespread during the Roman empire, the three great monotheistic religions, Judaism, Christianity and Islam, all placed constraints it. Through later centuries, excessive devotion to flowers has always smacked of paganism, although representations of flowers could be admitted as allegorical and symbolic, particularly in Islamic countries, where gardening survived after its decline in the West.

Above A detail from a wall painting at Pompeii, from the first century AD, shows an innocent delight in domesticated nature.

Persian gardens represent one of the oldest living traditions of symbolic garden design. Their forms were often transferred into the designs of Persian carpets. In the late Middle Ages, the idea of the enclosed garden, which is what the word 'paradise' literally means, was imported into Europe from the East to become part of the cult of the Virgin Mary. There was a consequent increase in the representation of flowers, especially the lily and the rose, reaching its climax in the late Gothic tapestries of France. In China, flowers and indoor trees (such as peach and tangerine) have ritual and seasonal significance, rather like the Christmas tree, which in the West is the best-known example of the ritual use of plants in the house.

The gardens of the Italian Renaissance are gradually offering up to historians their many layers of symbolic meaning. For instance, the famous gardens of the Villa d'Este at Tivoli, made in the 1590s, are an allegory of the creation of the world. In Renaissance gardens, the ancient pagan view of nature as a source of sexual energy was allowed a certain freedom. Grottoes became a favourite garden feature, not only providing a cool and private place but also allowing for a display of rare shells and minerals, illustrating the abundance of nature.

Gardens frequently act as what the French historian Michel Foucault called 'heterotopias' – real places that nonetheless offer a vision of a parallel universe where things are better than in everyday life. As they are normally individual and personal creations rather than professional ones, these private thoughts can remain on a subconscious level. The English landscape architect Geoffrey Jellicoe (1900–96) found his inspiration in the psychological studies of C. J. Jung and believed that gardens give access to the collective unconscious.

The 1940s and 1950s in the United States carried forward the unity of houses and gardens in a loose, informal version of the modern style that went with increasingly informal lifestyles. The title of the book written in 1955 by the American garden designer Thomas Church (1902–78),

Gardens are for People, conveys this message of living at ease with nature. The book encapsulates the belief that a sound structure of design principles would help nature to find expression, without the need for historic styles and conventional precedents.

On the larger scale of designed landscapes, nature has interacted fruitfully with modern art and design ever since the idea of a distinctly modernist landscape emerged in the interwar period. This has tended to imply a reversion to the formal elements of design, such as straight lines and grids, which are often considered 'unnatural' but which provide a matrix of geometry that can call forth the geometric and formal qualities of nature itself. Such design practice emphasises the double coding in nature, which can be interpreted either as chaos or as order, since elements of both are always present. Kathryn Gustafson, a contemporary American landscape designer based in London and Paris, has employed symbolism in the landscaping of the headquarters of the cosmetics group L'Oréal in Paris, based appropriately on the female body. The private garden designed by the American architectural critic Charles Jencks in Dumfriesshire, Scotland, in the mid-1990s, is a large-scale attempt to illustrate his interpretation of contemporary scientific thought, similar in its didactic purpose to the projects of the Renaissance.

from inside to outside

The art of dwelling involves relationships with fellow humans, and the ideal of the detached suburban house, pretending to be isolated from other people, has often been criticised as antisocial and wasteful of space. Houses in terraces prevent such a feeling of fragmentation. Complexes of houses with private courtyards and shared entrance areas off the main highway have captured the imagination of many architects, who see in them the kind of relationship of parts to a larger whole that is exhibited in nature. A housing scheme by the Danish architect Jørn Utzon (1918–) – also the author of the Sydney Opera House – has been described as 'arranged like flowers on the branch of a cherry tree, turning towards the sun from each flower's particular position'.

It is not easy to rationalise the criteria for naturalness in planning. It requires an understanding that rules are important, but that they should also at times be broken to prevent monotony – a paradox that is hard to enshrine in a legal system. The Picturesque doctrine of planning that developed in England in the early nineteenth century, seeking to bring nature into domestic design, has political implications when applied in modern society. It requires people to take responsibility for communal decisions that recognise the quality of collective life, as well as the rights of individuals. The best settlement plans have a combination of order and disorder that the French novelist Stendhal, writing about England, called 'le carefully careless'.

In the United States, the monotony of many suburban developments, where the houses are all designed with the same income level and conventional family structure in mind, is increasingly seen as a cause of social discontent. This can be remedied by combining variety with an active pursuit of beauty and a healthy lifestyle, less dependent on the car. Thus the design of housing can contribute to solving the problems of pollution and over-consumption by reintroducing people to the pleasures of home and community. The reciprocity of house and nature, inside and outside, individual and collective are all systems and relationships that are analogous to the processes of nature, allowing for structured change and flexibility. Nature means not only trees, flowers and water, but also a tuning device to transform chaos into order.

Above 'Le Palais Idéal du Facteur Cheval' at Hautrives, France, was built by Ferdinand Cheval, a postman who collected stones when making his rounds. On his death in 1924 he had completed a monument of the wildest fantasy in his garden.

Transparent architecture provides one way of dwelling in nature, by reducing the sense of a barrier between indoors and outdoors. Japanese houses have always paid attention to the presence of nature, while maintaining a strong formal language of architecture. The developing technology of glass in modern architecture, in the hands of architects such as Mies van der Rohe, creates a paradox in which nature is enhanced by the most sophisitcated forms of culture, allowing the illusion of being at one with nature outside while fully enclosed within walls of glass. The current fashion for conservatories has more to do with seeing nature outside than cultivating it inside, so that a glazed addition to a house can give an added sense of freedom. Houses can be planned in many ways to let nature in, and the division of the Sonoma House, by Joan Halberg, into a number of separate pavilions prevents it from dominating the landscape.

Clockwise from top A glass room at Courtney Drive, Hampstead, north London, 1996, by The Architects' Practice; a traditional setting for the Japanese tea ceremony; The Farnsworth House, by Mies van der Rohe, 1945–51; Sonoma House, Stewart's Point, Sonoma, California, by Joan Halberg.

Rather than contemplating nature at a distance, an alternative strategy is to bring it into an active relationship with the house. This can be done by building around what is already there, as in the Saul Bass house – the twentieth of the famous California 'Case-Study' houses of the post-war years – which integrates nature to the extent of building around an old stone pine. Similarly, the Empie House in Arizona incorporates huge boulders that would be hard to shift even if one wanted to. This kind of framing helps to draw attention to nature as a special feature. A ruin-effect garden wall recalls the sense of real ruins where nature begins to take over. In a conservatory, culture is usually in charge and nature is subordinated to design, with carefully chosen and displayed plants in their containers. Perhaps, one day, these will grow so big that nature will take over the conservatory too.

Clockwise from top The Empie House, Carefree, Arizona, by Charles Johnson, 1982; a historic conservatory at La Serre de Sagan; a wall imitates a ruin and lets in nature through the gap; the Saul Bass house, Altadena, California, by Buff, Straub and Hensman, 1958.

Natural materials can play an important part in creating the character of an interior, not just in the conventional uses of stone or timber but also in drawing attention – by means of exaggeration and strangeness – to the difference between nature and civilisation. Unexpected scale is one way to achieve this, as with the spectacular pine logs used in this Finnish ski cabin. Using raw materials in unexpected places is another way to create the same effect: although wooden baths are common in Japan, they are still a remarkable occurrence in London. Stone can be used effectively on a large scale, especially if it is already on the site, as Frank Lloyd Wright discovered on Edgar Kaufmann's estate in Pennsylvania. In a more eccentric take on the concept of nature in the home, a floor of pebbles provides a textural stimulus for feet.

Clockwise from top A novel floor of small, loose pieces of stone in a house in Paris; a ski cottage in Finland by Jukka Sirén; a minimalist London bathroom, with cedar wood bath, by Simon Conder Associates, 1997; the fireplace at Frank Lloyd Wright's Falling Water, Pennsylvania, 1935–39.

Mud is a practical and versatile building material, often available where timber and stone are lacking. Although it has long been considered a low-class material, architects and travellers have begun to value mud buildings in different parts of the world (like this extraordinary adobe church in New Mexico) for their sense of belonging and their effectiveness in climate control. The present revival of interest in mud buildings owes much to Hassan Fathy, who pioneered the rediscovery of traditional building techniques in Egypt. Even in Britain, as building regulations become more flexible, it is also now possible once more to build new structures in unconventional natural materials. This merely continues a long tradition of building with mud, as illustrated in this cob cottage in South Devon. Earth sheltering, seen in Cullinan's Visitor Centre in Aberdeenshire, is another way of using the thermal and visual properties of earth, in conjunction with other forms of structure.

Above Mud building in England: a cob cottage at Sherford, South Devon.
Left A mud-brick skyscraper: the Bayt Musallem, Shibam, Yemen.

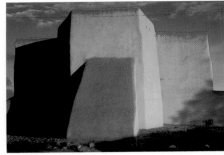

Above A domed roof by Hassan Fathy at New Gourna, Egypt.
Right Traditional adobe church, and living room in the Owings House, Jacona, both in New Mexico, USA.
Below Turf roof at a visitor centre in Aberdeenshire, by Edward Cullinan Architects.

nests and habitats |

Right Lake created by
Charles Jencks and
Maggie Keswick, southern
Scotland, early 1990s.
Below right Waterland,
Connecticut, USA,
a transformation of a
gravel pit by designer
Janis Hall, 1987.
Below Bridge of grass at
Saihoji-Moco, Kyoto,
Japan, a traditional
garden element.

The garden and the landscape have long been a place
where the artist or designer can work with nature to
send messages and alter perceptions. The development
of 'land art' in the 1960s gave a new status to this
practice. It was often inspired by the reverential attitude
to the natural world found in eastern religions, which
encourage careful and highly structured interventions
in nature. In such cases the effect is often gained by
some kind of paradox, by contradicting the expected,
as in the grass bridge in a Japanese temple garden.
'Waterland', paradoxically, is not made of water but
of undulating waves of grass, which reflect the forms
created by glacial action in the surrounding
countryside. It is best seen late in the day when the low
light casts shadows across the garden. In the same
spirit, Chris Drury's beautiful whirlpool transforms
stone into water, while Charles Jencks's cosmological
diagram exemplifies the curved, folded and wave-like
order of the universe in the grand tradition of
Renaissance emblematic gardening.

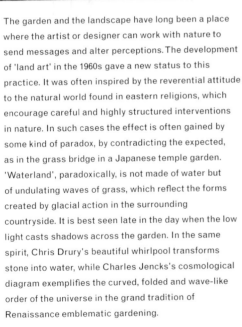

Above Senior tree house:
the seventeenth-century
timber-framed tree house at
Pitchford Hall, Shropshire.
Right Ease among the trees
in Ibiza: a platform
supported on the trunks
of trees growing
beside the house.

The idea of living up a tree may seem delightful or comical, but among certain civilisations of the past it was a good way of finding security. There are few natural experiences more pleasant than swaying gently with the breeze in a tree house, sheltered by leaves overhead and detached from the mundane world beneath. It may not be necessary to have all the comforts which Sir Thomas Lipton obviously enjoyed a century ago; indeed these seem somewhat incongruous in such a natural setting. Like many garden buildings, the Pitchford Hall tree house is a place for retreat from the cares of life. Few summer houses are up trees, however, and few tree houses are built so four-square and solid. In mid-nineteenth century Paris, a suburban restaurant, called l'Arbre de Robinson after Robinson Crusoe, served meals on a series of tree platforms. 'Robinson' still exists as a place-name, although the tree itself has gone.

Left A tree house in India.
Below Sir Thomas Lipton's tree house at Ossidge, Enfield, near London, c.1900.

nests and habitats |

Clockwise from top Shell-work detail from A La Ronde, Exmouth, designed and decorated from 1798; pebble decoration at Uggeshall, Suffolk, late nineteenth century; shell decoration inside a new grotto at Kerdalo, Brittany, made for Prince Peter Wolkonsky; exquisite pebble decoration in the Villa Litta, near Milan, 1520–30.

With their range of colours and shapes, pebbles and shells have great decorative potential – as evidenced by the exquisite pebble decoration in the nymphaeum of the Villa Litta near Milan. Accretions of small shells were often assembled to make imitation trees or flowers or, in some of the more spectacular grottoes, birds, beasts and monsters. Grottoes were part of the tradition of Renaissance garden design, providing a change of mood away from the sun, and their inspiration has led to home-made versions of the fantasy. Elizabeth and Jane Parminter were cousins who travelled to Italy together. On their return they built a remarkably original house, A La Ronde, which they decorated over the years not only with shells but also with seaweed and feathers. The use of pebbles in vernacular building is a more practical affair, but there is still a positive pleasure to be had in the imaginative folk art of cottages such as this one in Uggeshall, Suffolk.

In the domestic environment, water is a luxury which
can be enhanced through many different architectural
treatments – from the naturalistic to the highly artificial.
Frank Lloyd Wright chose to build over a waterfall in
the woods of Pennsylvania, while the gardens of the
Alhambra display water, which is both symbolic of
the rivers of paradise and cooling in a hot climate.
Contemporary architects use water as an additional
decorative element that has the ability to soothe and
to reflect light. A private pool need not be another hole
in the ground, as the rooftop swimming tank by Rem
Koolhaas shows. Contrast this with Georg Grotenfelt's
timber and glass sauna, and you have the whole gamut
of contemporary civilisation, from the height of artifice
to the least altered state of nature. The sauna is a
deliberate restatement of traditional forms, a building
apart from the main house, in accordance with long-
standing Finnish tradition.

nests and habitats |

Above Rooftop pool of
the Villa dall'Ava, Paris,
designed by Rem Koolhaas.
Right Lakeside sauna
by the Finnish architect
Georg Grotenfelt, 1982.
Below Pool in a house by
the Mexican architect
Luis Barragán.

Right The lesser masked weaver bird (*Ploceus intermedius*) builds its nest.
Below Cocoon lounge: a womb-like interior from the 1960s.

In the world's imagination, the strongest image of security against the hostile elements must surely be the Inuit igloo, whether built in a circle with blocks of ice or from other materials. The need for security in a house can be expressed architecturally with the same sense of intuition as that used by birds in building their nests. Soft, round, enclosing forms are comforting, suggesting security in a dangerous world, even when there is a view to the outside. Such forms are seldom encountered in the conventional house because they can readily be built only in a completely ductile material such as mud or concrete. Nevertheless, they seem for most people to epitomise the idea of 'home as security'.

Ushida Findlay's Soft and Hairy House, in Tokyo, was built for two architectural journalists who wanted a home based around Salvador Dali's statements about the architecture of the future. The pod (seen on the right in the picture) symbolically represents a child, protected between two recumbent parents, whose outline is represented in the overall plan.

Above Soft and Hairy House, Tokyo, by Ushida Findlay, 1993.
Left Interior of an Inuit dwelling in the Arctic region of Canada.

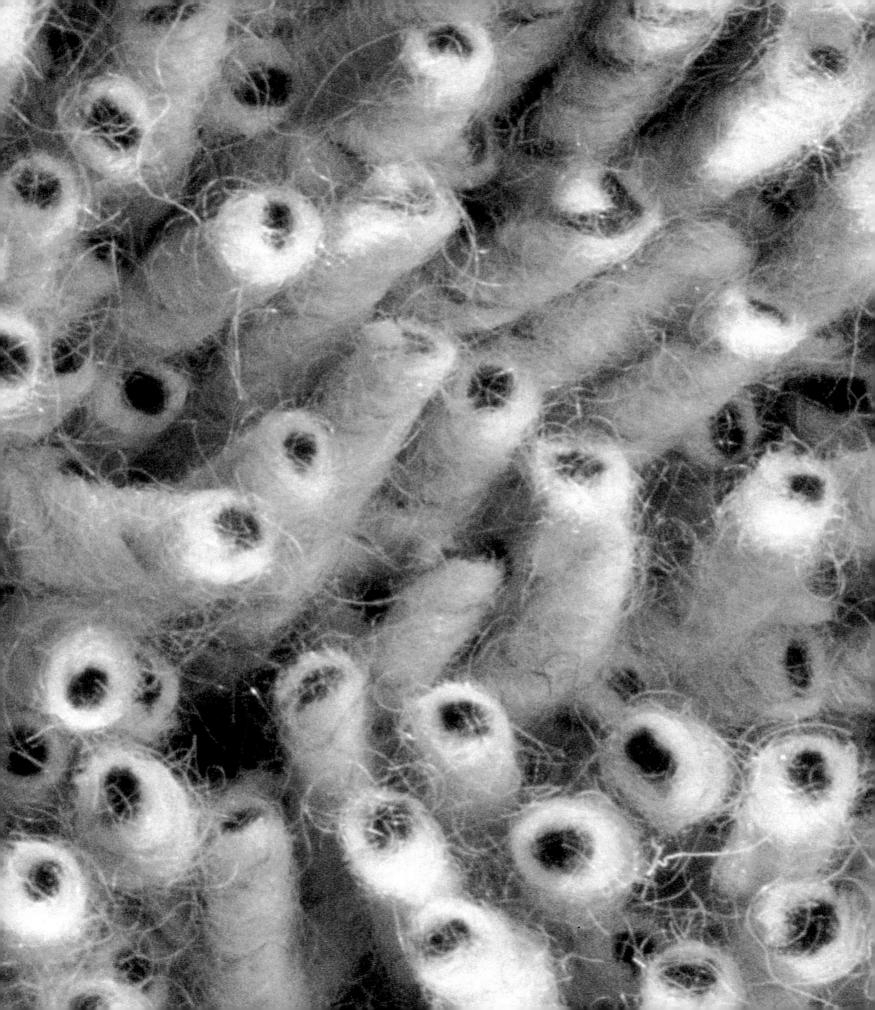

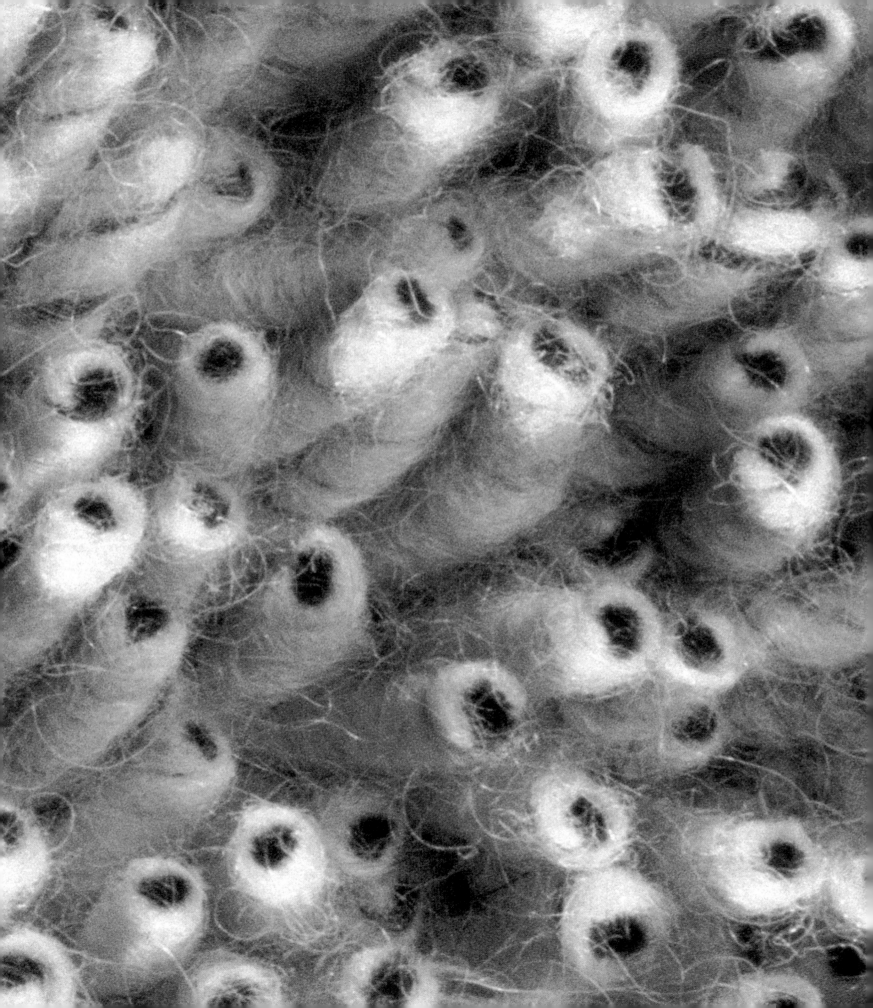

House furnishings and small articles of daily use are an important part of the coded language of design that we all use – consciously or not – to establish our relationship with the world. Designers and consumers can select from the imagery of nature to convey a wide range of messages as well as to meet practical needs. If we want them to, these objects can carry us back in time – baskets, spoons, cups and bowls from early civilisations are not very different from our own – and although we have many alternative materials, there is still pleasure to be had in using a horn spoon or a willow basket. Part of that pleasure comes from knowing that we have selected these products deliberately from a range of choices in order to affirm something we believe in, rather than accepting them as the only thing available.

creature comforts

The different interpretations of nature in decorative art is a fascinating subject. People may justify design in terms of its 'naturalness' without being aware of the complexity of nature and its capacity for contradicting itself. Naturalness can be manifested through an infinity of choices, depending on the way that nature is viewed. It cannot be defined in terms of any particular style of design. The ability to interpret nature through design cannot be instilled through training; it is a personal response.

Above In basket making, materials and process work together to create their own visual form.
Previous page Carpet by Liset van der Scheer, made from triple-strand yarn.

patterns from nature

The idea of adapting patterns from nature runs through all historical periods, although during the twentieth century it has been against the fashion for extreme simplicity. The geometrical ordering of leaves and flowers in nature is an invitation to the eye to see rhythms and two-dimensional relationships, while the techniques of weaving and printing by their very nature tend to encourage symmetry and repetition. These repeats, which may involve mirror symmetries or vertical steps of half a repeat-height, give a structure to the design that is not found in the natural world, but which still acts as a valuable diagnostic device for seeing nature's hidden structure and scale.

The renewed enthusiasm for William Morris in the 1960s arose from the fact that his career as designer, poet and political thinker was bound up in an attempt to restore the values of nature to everyday life. His wallpapers and fabrics were successful in spreading a particular quality of innocence, although the designs are far from naive. Morris knew the history of pattern design, but unlike other Victorian design reformers who turned to harsh lines and colours in their revolt against over-naturalistic portrayals of nature, he knew how to keep a sense of freshness and was sceptical of material progress.

A more extreme version of Morris's stylised naturalism can be found in the abstract quality of Turkish carpets. These patterns are concerned with organising the eye into seeing certain relationships of scale, outline and rhythm, and then adding the parts together to make a whole. As far as is possible in any man-made thing, they follow the infinite regression of scale in nature. It is in this set of relationships, infinitely varied but never random, that the living quality of nature is to be found.

There have been numerous notable designers of nature-based patterns during the twentieth century. The French painter Raoul Dufy (1877–1953) expressed a sophisticated but uncomplicated love of nature in his textile designs, used for furnishing and dresses, which employed flattened leaf and flower forms, usually on a large scale. Similarly, the Austrian architect Josef Frank (1885–1967) developed a range of brightly coloured textiles for the company Svensk Tenn. Based on slightly naive renderings of fruit and flowers, these provided an exuberant counter-balance to the austerity of modernism. His designs for textiles and wallpapers are still being produced in Sweden.

Printed textiles form a vast field of production, ranging between the craft studio and the mass market. Traditional flower patterns seldom disappear entirely, but at the fashionable end of the market they reappear from time to time in new guises. The 1960s saw many alternative treatments of nature, from giant floral motifs made possible by screen-printing to more subtle, abstract evocations of the mood of landscape and the different seasons. 'Flower-power' was manifested in over-scaled flat-coloured designs in the brightest possible colours, and by the end of the 1960s there was a conscious revival of Art Nouveau in textiles and wallpapers, bigger and brighter than the first time round. In the 1990s, textile designers failed to reawaken to the potential of repeat pattern as a way of reproducing the quality of nature. However, at the very end of the decade there are signs of a revival, exemplified by the Glasgow company Tim'rous Beasties, with its slightly surreal use of insect and animal imagery in textiles and wallpapers.

Since Europe became aware of Turkish and Persian carpets, floor coverings have made varied use of natural forms. In the eighteenth century, abstraction was exchanged for more literal renderings of nature, controlled within a classical outline. These were a way of showing off the design skills of the carpet weavers, as well as meticulous technique and high-quality dyeing. The development of machine looms for carpets made any form of design more reproducible, although the restrained taste of the early nineteenth century was lost. As the historian Nikolaus Pevsner wrote about some of the carpets from the Great Exhibition of 1851: 'We are forced to step over bulging realistic scrolls and into large, unpleasantly realistic flowers; it seems unbelievable that the teachings of Persian carpets should have been so completely forgotten.'

Above Willow Boughs wallpaper, designed by William Morris in 1887.

William Morris and other designers of the Arts and Crafts movement began to develop alternative ways of presenting nature in carpets, with flat pattern and a more structured overall design. The twentieth century demanded a different approach, and rugs produced between the wars, if not entirely abstract, often had large leaves drawn in outline. An example is the work of the American designer Marion Dorn (1899–1964), who was based in London in the 1920s and 1930s.

More recently, texture has become more important than pattern in floor covering. The Austrian-American architect Bernard Rudofsky (1905–88) proposed that people should remove their shoes indoors and have floors designed to give tactile stimulation to the feet, such as they might experience outdoors in the wild. Nature can be evoked by shag pile, or by the rough texture of sisal matting, which itself has the 'natural' quality of not being artificially coloured.

the perfection of workmanship

For William Morris, the process of coming closer to nature via the applied arts within the home was bound up with the rejection of Victorian ideas of social status and all that they implied in terms of ostentation and meaningless objects. Nature and culture were in opposition to each other, and, for Morris, culture had to give way in order for nature to regain its rightful position. The American housing reformer Catherine Bauer looked back from 1935 to the turn of the century and noted how 'there was a vague sort of idea, just gaining foothold, that "good taste" had something to do with simplicity. Some of the bric-a-brac and perhaps one set of curtains and one layer of carpet were dispensed with.'

The architect C. F. A. Voysey used forms that sometimes have a close affinity to Art Nouveau. His designs were more radically simplified than Morris's, however, and were based on a religious faith that Morris did not share. Voysey wrote that designers 'should each use their God-given faculties, and if they have thoughts worth expressing, the means to express them sufficiently are, and always have been, at hand. Not that we need shut our eyes to all human efforts, but we should go to Nature direct for inspiration and guidance. Then we are at once relieved from restrictions of style and period, and can live and work in the present with laws revealing always fresh possibilities.' Voysey, like the other pioneers and followers of modernism, was opposed to designing from precedent. In his case, this was not because a completely new style was required for a new century, but because nature provided all that was needed for inspiration; it made such self-consciousness not only unnecessary, but actually wrong.

The simple forms of Voysey's furniture, and the white-painted rooms that he designed for them to be seen in, are similar in character to the designs of the Shakers, where tradition and modernism meet without conflict. These small communities, who followed the vision of Mother Ann Lee, became established in the eastern United States in the late eighteenth century. Bringing the design of everyday things such as chairs, tables and beds into line with a profound belief about the meaning of the world, they produced a distinctive style with a timeless appeal. As the Anglo-Sinhalese art historian Ananda Coomaraswamy commented: 'That the Shakers were doctrinally Perfectionists is the final explanation of the perfection of Shaker workmanship; or, as we might have said, of its "beauty".' As part of their understanding of the spiritual nature of the world, the Shakers understood the subtle difference between an unforced intuitive inspiration from nature and an over-mechanical or over-imitative one. As they put it, that beauty is best which is 'peculiar to the flower or generative period', that is to say, which captures nature in its potential coming-into-being, rather than the beauty 'which belongs to the ripened fruit and grain'.

Without the spiritual vision to guide the design and its execution, imitations of Shaker pieces, like imitations of Voysey, lose much of their meaning. The special quality of the genuine examples comes through a holistic combination of design, materials and making process that gives a series of connected signals to the mind of the viewer, arousing a particularly sensitive response of sympathy and gratification. If this expectation is aroused but not fully satisfied – as may happen in the case of designs or objects that are made as copies without a thorough sympathy for the original, or with short-cuts for economy in materials or workmanship – the result can be merely sentimental or kitsch. The difference between success and failure is a narrow one, depending on the total quality of the object.

Rather than face this danger, modernism has tended towards austerity and simplicity, in which it may achieve a perfect counterpart to nature, but equally may achieve the opposite. In chair design, for example, there are shared aspects of modern furniture – like lightness in weight and appearance – which can be achieved equally well with timber or with steel tubing. The vocabulary of classic modern furniture covers a range of references to nature, from the natural cow hides and zebra skins used by Le Corbusier and Charlotte Perriand (1903–) on their famous chairs and *chaise basculant* launched in 1928, to the birch plywood of Alvar Aalto and the biomorphic ('life-shaped') curves of the American designers Charles and Ray Eames (1907–78; 1912–88), and Eero Saarinen (1910–61). Another strand of modern furniture design, which returned more directly to the past, emerged in Sweden and Denmark in the 1940s and 1950s with reworkings of 'classics' such as the ladder-back chair and Windsor chair; it was seen in Italy, too, in the Superleggera chair by Gio Ponti (1892–1979), with its thin wooden frame and sisal seat. These in their turn have become 'classics', favoured by contemporary minimalist designers to give a 'natural' look.

Left The simplicity of the Shaker style is seen in the Nurse Room at Hancock Shaker Village in Massachusetts.

In recent years, particularly among British designers, there has been a revival in one-off, craftsman-made furniture, where the overall form is often very simple and modern but special attention is given to the wood grain of veneers or solid timber. This can be seen in the furniture of John Makepeace (1939–) and his pupils at Parnham Manor, or the work of Alan Peters (1933–), who trained with Edward Barnsley, a maker in direct continuity with the Arts and Crafts movement. Richard La Trobe Bateman (1938–) is a furniture maker who has specialised in pieces that use timber on a heroic scale, while David Colwell (1944–), who comes from an engineering background, has employed sustainably grown timber scantlings, bent under steam, to produce elegant folding chairs. There are other much more expressive pieces, some with organic curves, and some – like the furniture of the French designer Philippe Starck (1949–) – which deliberately play with wood's 'as found' quality. Wood is such a useful material that to exclude it for long from the modern palette would be perverse. What has changed is the way of treating it. Instead of the traditional cabinet-maker's care, the British designer Jim Partridge (1953–), for example, has experimented with a much more tactile approach, involving carefully controlled burning and shaping. Others have made wood appear like driftwood, in which the grain is brought out by exposure and rough treatment so as to achieve a special beauty that layers of polish would hide.

Certain states of nature have become preferred metaphors for modern good taste. During the 1970s, a period of introspection and uncertainty about the world, earth tones became particularly popular, although they were often found in close conjunction with the most extreme and 'unnatural' colours left over from the 1960s. They extended through domestic objects to fashion and interior decoration, and even today the imagery of the farmhouse kitchen – with terracotta and stoneware jars, timber beams and stripped pine furniture – remains an emblem of nature.

fashioned in nature's image

Pots are among the oldest artefacts. The moulding of shapes out of clay is part of the Creation myth in certain cultures, and has the quality of a primal act. Pottery brings together the elements earth, air, fire and water to make a transformed substance that cannot go back to its original clay.

Ceramics can imitate nature in various ways, offering a background for the depiction of animals or plants, as demonstrated exquisitely by Chinese pottery and porcelain. Ceramics can mimic certain natural forms directly, accurately reproducing natural surfaces such as shiny animal skin, fruit or tree bark. Eighteenth-century tableware in majolica (coloured glazed earthenware) was often made in imitation of fruits and vegetables, slightly oversized and charmingly exaggerated.

The European tradition of decorative arts since the High Renaissance is based on rather different ideas of competing with nature, in terms of both technique and imagery. The French naturalist and potter Bernard Palissy (c.1519–90) produced mottled, lifelike glazes on lizards and snakes that look as if they were moulded from actual creatures. These were less pieces for normal use than objects of wonder. With the growth of a middle class in Europe in the seventeenth and eighteenth centuries, there was an increasing diversity of ceramic ware. The Rococo style of the mid-eighteenth century made free use of natural imitation, with an informality and charm derived from the Chinese. The Chelsea porcelain factory in London made plates with relief vine leaves and life-sized painted butterflies, as well as tureens in the shape of melons and plates with accurate botanical specimens. Some of this exuberance was banished by the neo-classical taste of Josiah Wedgwood (1730–95) in the 1770s, and excessive naturalism in pottery, when it has recurred, has tended to be frowned on by taste-makers.

The design of light fittings offered great possibilities for those working in the Art Nouveau manner. A writer in *La Lumière Electrique* (1887) explained that 'the shape of the light bulb, following the curves of the spirally rolled filament, practically calls out to be surrounded by a flower, where it represents the pistil. Or it could be given the colour and shape of a piece of fruit. The plant world offers endlessly new and charming possibilities. The presentation of the bulb as a flower or a fruit tends to result in the plant motif being continued throughout the whole lamp.'

In these early years of electricity designers came up with some of the finest lighting fitments that have ever been created. In England, the designer W. A. S. Benson (1854–1924) specialised in the production of domestic metalwork, including early electric lamps whose copper shades are made like the individual petals of a flower. These were favoured by the architect C. F. A. Voysey for his interiors, and sold at the Parisian shop L'Art Nouveau, which gave the name to the European movement. Compared to candles and oil lamps, electric lighting gave a rather hard, cold effect. People were not used to having their rooms so brightly lit, so many fittings were designed to soften the quality of the light emitted. The imagery of nature combined with experiments in craft-made glass technology enabled this to happen.

The American Louis Comfort Tiffany (1848–1933) was inspired by the English Arts and Crafts movement to produce fine original decorative objects, specialising in glass with brilliant iridescent surfaces and shapes with a natural freedom, abstraction and informality. Emile Gallé (1846–1904) was working in Nancy in eastern France in the same period, establishing a local centre of Art Nouveau after learning the glassmaker's trade in Germany. Like Tiffany, he was inspired by plant forms and published several books on the subject. He made glass and metal pieces that were suitable for adaptation to the new technology of lighting, particularly with the use of translucent effects that softened the harshness of the bulb within.

After the fashion for Art Nouveau, there was a new appreciation of the qualities of machine production. In 1907 the German architect and artist Peter Behrens became design consultant to AEG, the largest German electrical company. His new designs were praised because they got away from the imitation of nature: 'Artistic form should rather illustrate the purpose of the object as clearly as possible, using expressive means that correspond to the characteristics of the given material. How unnatural ... the garland of leaves on the lantern of the old style of arc lamp appears to today's better-educated eye, how inept are the efforts to reproduce the graceful forms of delicate leaves in pressed metal.'

This change of direction has dominated the design of modern lighting, although nature has made an impact in less literal ways than it did during the Art Nouveau period. The Danish designer Poul Henningsen (1894–1967) realised that the geometrically simple shapes of modernism did not eliminate glare from the light source, as older light fittings had successfully done. He therefore developed more complex forms based on the quality of light, which nonetheless retained an overall purity. Henningsen's hanging lamp of 1926 has three opal glass shades, one inside the other, like a hanging flower bud, providing a softer light and making a more interesting visual form. The same principle was developed throughout his career, culminating in the Artichoke light of 1958. Made in white and in copper colour, the design maximises the reflected light while reducing glare.

The Anglo-Japanese contemporary designer, Isamu Noguchi (1904–88), has included light fittings in a diverse career. He took the Japanese tradition of a paper lantern strengthened with cane and between 1951 and 1966 devised many variations on this theme, using bamboo and metal supports. These pieces have a non-specific relationship to natural form, partly through their fragility and the tactile quality of the paper. The effect is very different to the unnatural quality of lighting produced from hard materials using pure geometric shapes.

Lighting design continues to operate between the poles of nature and industry, with some designs suggestive of organic form, while others employ pure geometry and straight lines. The light fittings of the Art Nouveau period are still inspirational today. A light does more than provide illumination – it can be an important contributor to the atmosphere of an interior. For the purpose of atmosphere, however, electric light has still not superseded the live naked flame of the candle.

Above Dish by Bernard Palissy, prodigious potter of Renaissance France. Left Emile Gallé's lamp, Aristolochia: Plante Carnivorée, makes a sinister companion in a room.

ecology and interior design

The ecological movement affects design at many levels. For the consumer, ecological issues can influence the choice of household furnishings as much as foodstuffs. Over the past twenty years they have shifted from being the concern of a few enthusiasts, to influencing the buying patterns of a large and articulate group of consumers. Recycled products – whether furniture from shredded plastics or crushed cans, textiles woven from discarded packaging, or the more familiar examples of recycled paper and salvaged building materials – are now much more widely available. Indeed, a recent review of businesses involved with recycling glass and paper into 'design' objects in the United States claimed that they might be artificially maintaining production levels of the waste that provides their raw material.

Recycling and its counterpart, production from sustainable resources, now have an important effect on the design of household goods, although there are sectors, such as electrical goods, which rely on the product being scrapped if it fails because it is impossible to mend. In looking for the right balance between luxury and austerity, we might surmise that society in developed countries is working through a crisis about its high living standards and their relationship to the problem of global sustainability. The benefits of finding such a balance have been articulated by the contemporary designer Ann Maes: 'A simple minimal design,' she writes, 'is not only more timeless than decorative or over-ornate styling, but it also builds a communicative bridge between the product and its users, with the added advantage of restoring visual peace and quiet to our environment.'

Nature presents a great variety of ground surfaces as an inspiration to the designer, from pebble beaches to the forest floor. These in turn can inspire the design of floor surfaces for the domestic interior. Pebbles inspired many modern artists, and in Natalie Woolf's photographic floor tiles they form a random abstract pattern with the kind of internal logic that natural arrangements tend to possess. The Crop Circles carpet by Amazed is a striking reference to a puzzling phenomenon of the late twentieth century, in which nature appears to design itself in bold geometric configurations. Japanese tatami mats are a traditional floor covering, well-suited to a culture in which shoes are removed indoors and the texture of the floor becomes as important as its visual contribution to the room. The architect C. F. A. Voysey designed many carpets for the Donegal Carpet Industry, a philanthropic enterprise in a poor part of Ireland intended to capture through lively modern designs the best traditional qualities of hand knotting and natural dyes.

Above Crop circle carpet by Amazed, 1998.
Right The rich texture of a forest floor.
Below Vinyl tile by Natalie Woolf Surface Design.

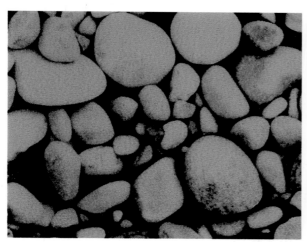

Left Japanese tatami mats.
Below The Donnemara,
a Donegal wool carpet by
C. F. A. Voysey, 1902.

creature comforts

104

creature comforts

Wall decorations imitate nature in a variety of forms, a favourite being those that make you feel you are out of doors when you are actually inside. Nobody is really supposed to be fooled by this, but the fictional version of nature sometimes turns out to be more suggestive than the real thing. In the time of the Roman emperor Augustus, the painter Ludius began a fashion for trompe l'oeil garden scenes of a delightful and informal character. In the Middle Ages, tapestries were the grandest form of room decoration and frequently included representations of landscape or gardens as a background to mythological scenes. Pattern designers can reproduce nature with formalised but recognisable forms. Voysey's pattern, Let us Prey, has a humorous message about the systems of nature, or perhaps the predatory character of church-goers. Patterns can also look beyond representation to the abstract forms suggested by the close-up structure of matter, creating an effect of liveliness and movement. This is the oldest kind of pattern, as well as the most modern.

Above C. F. A. Voysey, Let us Prey, design for wallpaper, *c.*1900.
Right Anonymous English wallpaper of 1959, reflecting the fashion for patterns based on atomic structures.

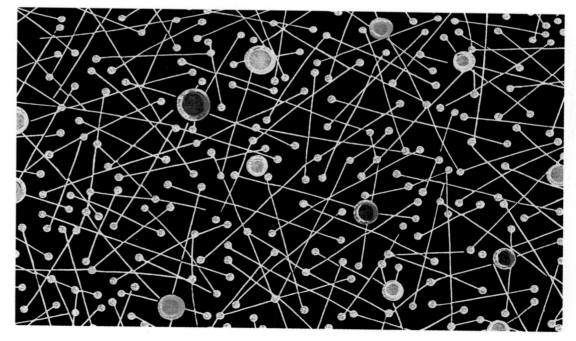

Above Roman wall painting
from the Villa of Livia, wife
of the emperor Augustus,
now in the Museo delle
Terme, Rome.

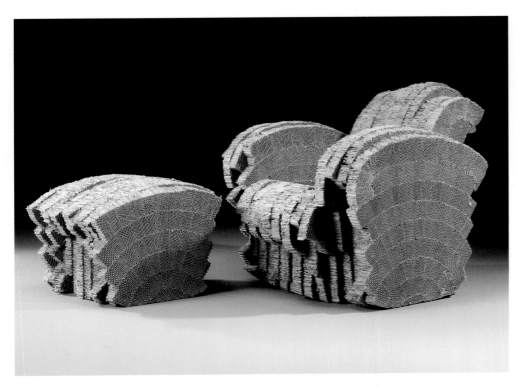

Chairs have a 'creaturely' quality by virtue of their adaptation to the shape of the human body. A good chair offers a wordless invitation to sit down and share its secrets. Like other kinds of furniture, chairs convey a variety of complex messages to those who have the inclination to listen. Eighteenth-century 'rustic' chairs were intended less for sitting (or so one might infer from their fragile but uncomfortable look) than as a component in a thematic decorative scheme based on *faux-naif* rusticity. Most chairs have a linear quality through which their visual character is immediately conveyed, as seen in Ron Arad's LoopLoop chair of woven stainless steel. On a more basic level, chairs offer the opportunity to use a variety of natural materials for structure or covering. Leather and hides are functional and gratifying to the touch, and fake zebra has become a popular fabric, replacing the real zebra popular in the 1930s. Chairs seldom take their place among natural objects as easily as Mari-Ruth Oda's stoneware Sit-tables.

creature comforts

Clockwise from top Little Beaver chair and ottoman by architect Frank Gehry, made of recycled cardboard; a modern interior in Melbourne, Australia; eighteenth-century English 'rustic' Rococo chair; Ron Arad's LoopLoop chairs, 1993; Sit-tables in stoneware by Mari-Ruth Oda.

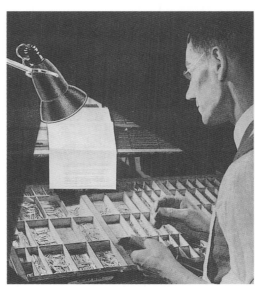
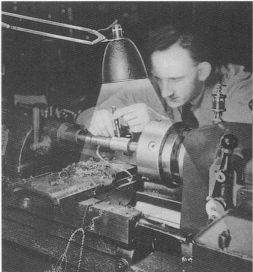

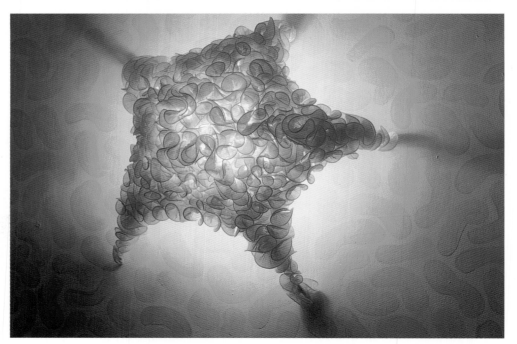

Lighting is a versatile field for invention, where function and metaphor work hand in glove. Containers for light can resemble many of nature's containers, especially those that are fragile and translucent. Ayala Sperling Serfaty, designer of the Baby Starfish light, got her inspiration when swimming in the Red Sea. The anglepoise lamp has a very different source: a design classic dating from the 1930s, it is based on the relationship of the bones and muscles in the human arm and employs a system of springs that enables the two hinged sections to remain in place. Lighting is rich in meaning, its magic glow influencing the surrounding space and drawing the eye towards it, as can be seen in the light designed by Charles Rennie Mackintosh for Hill House. Although purists argue that a light fitting should be all but invisible, it can benefit greatly from having a character of its own, as do the MaMo Nouchies lights illustrated here.

Clockwise from top The anglepoise lamp, a design classic still very much in use today; Gaku light, 1998, from the MaMo Nouchies range by Ingo Maurer; physalis seed pods create natural lanterns; wall light from the drawing room at Hill House, Helensburgh, Scotland, by Charles Rennie Mackintosh, 1902; Baby Starfish light by Ayala Sperling Serfaty.

creature comforts

Clockwise from top left
Pumpkin by Kate
Malone; dish by Janice
Tchalenko and Roger
Law; ebonised wood
vessel by Jim Partridge.

Vessels and containers are among the objects found in
nature that can most readily be adapted for human use.
A scallop can be served at table in its own shell, while
the rind of a fruit or the shell of an egg are wrappings of
the most ingenious kind: disposable and biodegradable,
they contain a unit of convenient size for transport and
consumption – no wonder that arguments proving a
grand design of the world are so convincing. Dishes and
bowls evoke a variety of natural forms. Some are self-
evident, like Kate Malone's pumpkin; some pictorial, like
Janice Tchalenko and Roger Law's fish dish; and some
referential in a more abstract way, like Jim Partridge's
vessel of ebonised wood, which uses one natural
material to evoke another kind of nature. Alvar Aalto's
Savoy vase, designed in 1936, presents, in its wavy line,
a diagram of natural form that does not need to be
pinned to a specific reference. People have seen in it
the outline of a typical lake from Aalto's native Finland,
but Aalto himself – perhaps to tease them and to leave
open the field of interpretation – called it 'an Eskimo
woman's leather breeches'.

Left Savoy vases by Alvar
Aalto, 1936.

As the fashion historian France Borel writes: 'It is by their categorical refusal of nakedness that human beings are distinguished from nature ... The body is tamed continuously; social custom demands, at any price – including pain, constraint, or discomfort – that wildness be abandoned.' However, even though the very existence of clothes asserts a separation from nature, fashion is intimately connected to nature in terms of its repertoire of materials, design motifs and meanings.

We know that the functional aspect of clothing, although of primary importance in protecting us from heat or cold and affording us a degree of privacy, is not the only motivation for clothing. This is particularly evident in those climates that do not necessitate the wearing of clothes. One might think

fur and feathers

that it would be possible simply to do without any kind of apparel, but instead, items are worn just as much for symbolic reasons as for comfort or protection. Clothes are a way of communicating who a person is within the social group, and for differentiating different social groups from each other.

the language of fashion

The symbolic value of clothing may seem removed from an ideal of natural simplicity, but nature has plenty of precedents for differentiation of gender as a primary symbolic function of dress. The idea of similarity and difference existing side by side is one of the underlying principles of nature, and styles of dress continue to work on this principle.

The French anthropologist Claude Lévi-Strauss (1908–) records of the Caduveo of Brazil: 'In order to be a man, one had to be painted; whoever remained in a natural state was no different from the beasts.' Among native North Americans, Lévi-Strauss found that clothes symbolise the transition from nature to culture. People in modernised societies may be the first to try to escape this need to dress within such patterns of meaning, and it is true to say that the codes of social and economic class that were still evident in dress twenty or thirty years ago are beginning to disappear. However, a structure of meaning is still required, so the messages of gender and sexual attraction that clothes convey remain an important aspect of fashion. This may be the outcome of all forms of social existence, for, as the design historian John Harvey believes, 'clothing articulates a political will, both reinforcing the wearers and binding them to something larger, and not only inviting but exacting a certain form of attention from others'.

the colour of gender

The colours and forms of birds indicate the need for the male to make a display in order to attract the attention of a mate. The female is usually less visible and more inclined to be coloured for camouflage while sitting on the nest. In the case of the peacock's brilliant plumage, it is the condition of the tail feathers that is thought to signal to the peahen whether or not the potential mate is a healthy specimen. A male's display is not necessarily always bright, however. Darwin noted the effect of black in the common blackbird: 'The males alone are black, whilst the females are brown or mottled; and there can hardly be a doubt that blackness in these cases has a sexually selected character ... With several birds, in which the male alone is black, and in others in which both sexes are black, the beak or skin about the head is brightly coloured, and the contrast ... adds greatly to their beauty.'

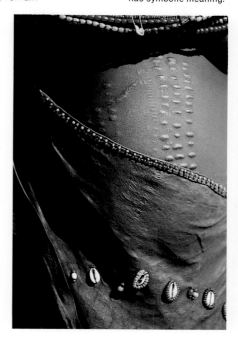

Previous page Black layered taffeta dress by Christian Dior, 1949. **Below** Cowrie shells, a sign of fertility, are sewn on to the dress of a Pokot woman from Cherangani, Kenya. Her scarified skin also has symbolic meaning.

Curiously, male clothing and fashion have also swung between extremes on this question, alternating between periods of 'display' fashion in metaphorical peacock feathers – such as the sixteenth-century court of Queen Elizabeth in England, or the eighteenth century in Europe – with periods of unassertive style, marked by conventionality and understatement. Black, in particular, has grown more dominant among groups that aspire to be arbiters of taste in design. As early as 1810, Goethe wrote in *Theory of Colours*: 'People of refinement have a disinclination to colours. This may be owing partly to weakness of sight, partly to the uncertainty of taste which readily takes refuge in absolute negation.' The most significant historical change occurred quite rapidly around 1830, when colours in male clothes became muted or disappeared altogether – a transformation that has never been significantly reversed, apart from a brief rebellion in the 1960s with 'flower power'. This was a fascinating moment in the history of fashion, when the conventions of male dress seemed on the point of breaking down.

Above For a brief moment in the 1960s, men were 'permitted' to wear colourful and decorative clothes, attire usually reserved for women. This couple is on parade in London's Carnaby Street in its heyday.

Men began to adopt many aspects of female attire. These included loose-fitting clothes, soft and impermanent fabrics such as cheesecloth, bright colours and floral patterns, which even the relatively conventional man might dare to wear in the form of a tie. Long hair was an important symbol of an altered masculinity, which in fact was a reversion to older forms. In their most intense form, the extremes of hippie dressing did not last very long, but the meaning of men's clothes could never again be taken for granted in quite the same way.

The lasting result of the 1960s upheaval was not that men began to dress like women, but that women began increasingly to dress like men, whether for leisure in jeans or for work in pinstripe skirts, trousers and jackets. Such levelling went with a widespread readjustment of gender roles and relationships as the consequences of feminism spread ever wider.

fashion and function

Gender relations are not, of course, the only determining factor in establishing the coded meaning of dress. Some kinds of dress are normally deemed to be specific to certain activities, notably sport, where a certain functionality is needed, and where new experiments into fabrics can be tried out. The need to wear highly visible clothing for certain team sports, made more pressing by the exigencies of television, has led to the development of a mode of clothing separate from the normal determinants of fashion, while at the same time beginning to infiltrate it.

The question raised by clothes is the same as that raised in other areas of design: do functionality and nature reinforce each other? The American social commentator Thorstein Veblen (1857–1929) wrote in *The Theory of the Leisure Class* (1901) about the complicated system of symbols by means of which fashion in his time was controlled. He believed that the chief way in which the middle and upper classes distinguished themselves from their so-called inferiors was to adopt forms of dress that made it clear that they could not do manual work. Such work would be too uncomfortable for a woman wearing a corset, or a man in formal dress. Veblen thought that this was a ridiculous reason for suffering a lifetime's discomfort from clothes, and felt that working people were able to dress and live more naturally, whatever other deprivations they may have suffered.

The Russian Revolution in 1917 offered an opportunity to display a different kind of fashion, unaffected by social class. The textile artist and clothing designer Varvara Stepanova (1894–1958) glorified working clothes as the most practical and rational form of dress, in her versions of overalls and boiler suits, while the stage designer Alexandra Exter (1882–1949) believed that revolutionary clothing should learn naturalness from Russian folk art and thereby differentiate itself from western-European designs. Nature was not stated as a source of design, but the Russian avant-garde shared Veblen's view that, in a commercial society, fashion was likely to be wasteful and irrational because of its need to change continuously, whereas nature offered better examples of change related to external factors.

Sports clothes, which Stepanova included in her design reform programme, have to be comfortable to wear for obvious reasons. They are, therefore, arguably more 'natural' than those manifestations of fashion that more evidently derive their forms from culture, and which are judged primarily on grounds of taste. In reality, convenience and comfort are mixed with other, more complex forms of symbolism and meaning. 'Natural' in the context of fashion is often taken to mean something quite different, for example, the rough textures of untreated cotton or the subtle colours that result from using vegetable dyes such as indigo, madder, cochineal or bog-myrtle.

The exhibition 'Are Clothes Modern?', which the architect Bernard Rudofsky presented at the Museum of Modern Art in New York in 1944, made contrasts between the simple directness of modern architecture and the irrationality of fashion at that time. Rudofsky declared that 'the day when fashion and fashion-makers will be forgotten like a nightmare – on this day we shall have made one big step toward a more intelligent way of living'. His prediction has not been entirely false, for most people today find that simple, comfortable and informal clothes are acceptable in a wide variety of situations. The fashion industry has not disappeared as a result, however; nor have people altogether lost an appetite for clothes that make a special point by their lack of functionality.

The development of new types of fabric appears, on the face of it, to be a move away from nature. The contemporary British hat designer Chrissij van den Munckhof (1962–), for example, uses a synthetic combination of polyurethane and nylon called 'Felvet', which combines the qualities of felt and velvet. She markets her work as 'one hundred percent unnatural'. The Japanese fashion designer Issey Miyake (1938–) works closely with textile designer Makkiko Minagawa to combine the qualities of traditional natural silks and cottons with aspects of synthetic materials. Whether or not synthetic fabrics should look and feel natural is largely a matter for the designer to decide. Nature has such a large repertory of colour and texture that it is hard to avoid corresponding to it in some respect. Moreover, 'naturalness' is not only a matter of look and feel but also relates to a wider context of use. Breathable waterproof fabrics such as Gortex have made a significant impact on leisure clothing, at a time when people expect their clothes to be lightweight but adaptable to different temperatures and weather conditions. Thus, paradoxically perhaps, unnatural fabrics make it easier to enjoy nature.

a natural form of dress

Flowers are the basis of the majority of textile pattern designs, and their small units are suitable to most forms of production, whether by embroidery, weaving or printing. The boldness of flower patterns for woven silks during the eighteenth century was astonishing and had the added dimension of textures raised and developed by the process of weaving. In England, in the silk designs of the Yorkshire woman Anna Maria Garthwaite, which survive from the 1740s, it is clear that new botanical discoveries were eagerly incorporated into pattern designs, while the customary presentation of the flowers as independent stems on a plain ground resembles the manner of botanical drawing and illustration. While using nature as a close reference, pattern designs were at the same time highly inventive in the free mixture of motifs and the variety of colours. This was the Rococo period, when the uninhibited depiction of nature had a brief moment of triumph before being suppressed by standards of 'correctness'.

In 1774, English textile producers were for the first time allowed by law to print on cotton, which had previously been prohibited as a way of protecting the linen, wool and silk trades. The result was a flood of calico (cotton) prints that were influenced by the Indian style of textile design, with small, less naturalistic motifs. These were derived from flowers, but sometimes abstracted into stars and dots. Little sprays of flowers and linear patterns resembling seaweed were popular designs, as can be seen in the pages of Barbara Johnson's *Album of Fashions and Fabrics* in the V & A Museum in London. She lived from 1738 to 1825, a period during which fashion became simpler and more informal, in line with the increasing interest in nature in the realm of ideas. Flower patterns have been reinvented many times to suit changing conditions. Among the most beautiful are those which the French painter Raoul Dufy, a lover of women and of flowers, devised initially for his countryman, the couturier Paul Poiret (1879–1944), who wanted to have more individual printed fabrics for his radically simplified clothes in the period just before the First World War. Poiret was the fashionable inheritor of the movement for dress reform in the years leading up to 1900. This was an important attempt to create an entirely different kind of relationship between clothes and nature, although the results were not intended to be glamorous. The Rational Dress Society was founded in England in 1881 and its pamphlet *Reasons for Reform in Dress* quoted William Morris's view that decoration was beautiful only if it accorded with nature. Women's clothes were unnatural, for 'not only are the true lines of Nature ignored but they are positively reversed ... A woman's waist in Nature's scheme is broad and flat. Are the bodies of most of the dresses we see calculated to set off this sort of figure? Are they not, on the contrary, designed expressly for a round waist, sloping in like the letter V from under the arms, thus contradicting Nature's lines directly?' Naturalness was expressed through a reduction in the number of clothes worn, the abandonment of restrictive undergarments such as tight-laced corsets, and the general avoidance of bright colours, display and 'artificiality'. The growth of outdoor activities for women, including bicycling and tennis, helped to introduce changes through the special types of clothing required for these activities.

Men's clothing was similarly affected, frequently receiving ridicule. Wool was favoured for its 'breathing' qualities, and science, in the person of Dr Gustav Jaeger of Stuttgart, who advocated woollen underwear, was allied to the commercial enterprise of the British Jaeger Clothing Company, founded in 1883 and still flourishing. The argument was that animal fibres were intrinsically more natural than vegetable ones (there were at the time no artificial yarns to complicate the dichotomy). George Bernard Shaw (1856–1950), a social and political progressive, adopted Jaeger's methods. In his desire to improve every aspect of life, by adopting a more 'natural' approach, he typified the 'dress reformer'.

Above Freedom through tennis: a cartoon by Ferd von Reznicek in Simplicissimus (1903) captures the early days of dress reform in conservative Austria.

The liberation of reform was achieved on the stage by the American dancer and choreographer Isadora Duncan (1878–1927). She scandalously performed her revolutionary Greek-style dancing wearing nothing but a loose tunic. Eccentricity was licensed for artists such as Gustav Klimt (1862–1918), who was photographed in a Viennese garden in a sack-like garment, or the English sculptor and designer Eric Gill (1882–1940), who gave up trousers before the First World War and wore a smock-like form of monk's habit. Meanwhile the Ballets Russes of Sergei Diaghilev (1872–1929), which arrived in Paris in 1909, encouraged an exotic naturalism, derived from the harem pants worn by women dancers in *Schéhérazade*.

from shepherdesses to punks

The delicate 'feminine' flower patterns of Laura Ashley, introduced about the time of the 1973 oil crisis, became a symbol of post-hippie opting-out from modernism in favour of nature. While this fashion was still widespread in 1981, Alison Lurie wrote about the 'English shepherdess look' in terms that repeat the hostile critique of rational and aesthetic dress as play-acting in the 1880s: 'As well as pretending to be country wear, these clothes are associated with innocence, youth and dainty femininity; they imply an interest in old-fashioned creative domestic pursuits: gardening, hand-weaving, jam-making. When they are worn in town, the message is "I don't really belong here, behind this desk or in this flat; my rightful place is in the garden of a rather large country house."'

Fortunately, the role of nature in fashion could not be limited to such simplistic equivalents. The launch of Issey Miyake's career as a designer in 1970 demonstrated the possibility of a new synthesis between old-fashioned *haute couture* and the pop styles of the 1960s, where the structures of the old formality were banished, but the craftsmanship remained. As the Japanese architect Arata Isozaki (1931–) wrote in 1978: 'Issey Miyake returns to the original state of clothing by flinging a single piece of fabric or a long sash-like material over the body. In this way the fabric makes itself self-evident without hampering its original shape ... [He] places a great significance on clothing which has been inherited from the past, including farm clothes and designs created through necessity.' His use of texture and colour, combined with a varied approach to the body and an ability to cross the gender gap, makes Miyake an exemplar of a way of designing in which nature is a standard of truth and quality.

Then, into the middle of the 1970s 'green dream' of late hippie and Laura Ashley style landed the bombshell of Punk, which could hardly have been more different: urban and brash with overt indications of sado-masochism. The overriding criteria was summed up by Elizabeth Wilson: 'What was important was that nothing should look natural'. Yet the 'Mohican' haircut, the tattoos and piercings, which unleashed aspects of street and club style that have had a powerful influence on fashion in the late 1990s, can be seen as more authentically connected to the 'nature' of primitive peoples than any number of ecological or retro styles.

If, as people believed, cities had turned into 'urban jungles', then a regression of clothing to primitive ways of communicating

Below By rejecting 'naturalness' in dress, Punk rockers in 1970s Britain invented a tribal language that employed many of the symbolic devices of primitive cultures.

group membership is not surprising. Counter-cultures in modern society express themselves through dress codes, whether these are hippie, skinhead or Punk. Often, there is no worked-out set of beliefs for the group, and the clothes, perhaps together with other social indicators like a certain style of music, become one of the principal ways of constructing the group identity. These variants on normal fashion have only ever been practised by a minority, but they usually succeed in attracting attention and may even become incorporated in *haute couture*. With the Punk style, there was a circularity of influence, originating from the British designer Vivienne Westwood (1941–), who has always stood outside the commercial fashion scene in London. These ideas became the origin of a street style, from which the French designer Jean-Paul Gaultier (1952–) and others then reincorporated aspects into high fashion.

The derivatives of Punk, including various aspects of sadomasochist dress, consciously play on the meanings of clothing and the body. They are irrational and in that sense anti-modern. The Viennese architect Adolf Loos (1870–1933) actually based his theory of *Ornament and Crime* (1909) on the assumption that the more advanced civilisations would leave behind the decoration of buildings and interiors in the same way that only 'criminals and degenerates' now practised body decoration. However, if he was correct about architecture, he was wrong about tattoos, which now form part of a firmly established counter-culture rather than being merely a fleeting phase.

'Fetishism' is a term from anthropology that describes the transference of emotional, magical or religious feeling from people to objects. These 'fetish objects' are not normally items of clothing, but there are nonetheless garments described in many mythologies that confer power on the wearer. In its modern usage, fetishism tends to refer to unusual styles of dress that express or substitute for 'abnormal' sexual desires and behaviour. These, for a long time the preserve of more or less hidden and suppressed minorities, have increasingly come into the open in a modified form as part of the repertory of fashion.

Fur and leather, both animal-derived clothing products, have always played an important role in fetishistic dress, perhaps because they create an ambiguity of life and death. John Harvey writes of black leather biker gear: 'It is raw: a way of wearing on top of your clothes what normally is underneath them, skin – except that it is not so much skin as hide … Depending on who wears the black leather, and in what situations, it may use its death-power and animal-power combined to add danger and charge to sexuality.' The founding text of masochism is the nineteenth-century Austrian novelist Leopold von Sacher-Masoch's *Venus in Furs*. Does the highly visible campaign against furs by animal rights activists give them an even greater aura of the forbidden? The use of corsets and tight lacing has a cult following, in defiance of the strictures of the dress reformers, and also made a return into high fashion in 1987 with Jean-Paul Gaultier's corset collection, made famous by the singer Madonna.

the symbolism of clothes

The dress reformers equated nature in dress with a form of functional rationalism, not unlike the parallel argument that was going on in architecture. This was a new way of looking at clothes, but although it has had a gradual influence, rational dress has never defeated its opposition: the practice and indulgence of fashion for its own sake. When it comes to something so intimately reflecting their own sense of identity as their clothes, people do not want to be purely rational all the time.

It will be interesting to see whether the long-established, coded differences between male and female dress begin to break down as feminism redefines the role of women and the sexes become more equal; whether the result will be a reversed pattern, with flamboyant males and reticent females; or whether the sense of difference will be eroded, in the same way that social class differences in clothing are so much less important than they were fifty years ago. A 'natural' model for dress and fashion will need to attend not only to the rational but also to the social and symbolic aspects of dress. The desire to play with these seems to be an essential aspect of human nature.

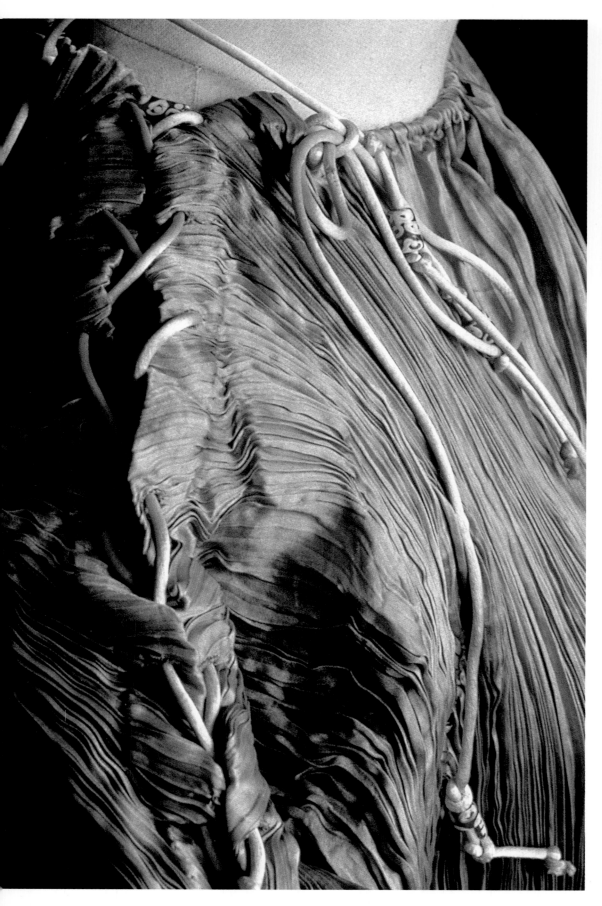

Tight and loose clothes reflect different conditions of nature. The looseness of Mariano Fortuny's famous pleated Delphos dresses, of 1906, seemed amazingly natural when launched into a world of artificial body shapes. The dresses' rippling lines and references to ancient Greek statuary also imbued them with a rich layer of meaning, however. The wooden bustier/corset by Hussein Chalayan is more a catwalk novelty than a practical garment, but it could evoke thoughts of Greek dryads – the nymphs who inhabited trees – and suggest the many visual and emotional comparisons between trees and people. Chalayan is known for his interest in pushing back the boundaries of form and cutting clothes in an 'architectural' way. Georgina Godley's Lumps and Bumps collection reverts to a Victorian concept of altering natural body shape by exaggeration. It stands in deliberate contrast to the mainstream of 'natural' fashion, which nevertheless controls body shape by setting up the ideal of the model's figure. In male street styles, tight and loose form a coded language. Skateboarding culture has developed an exaggerated bagginess of clothing, not unlike the Oxford bags of the 1920s (which also saw a revival in the very wide-cut trousers of the 1970s). While these fashions are ostensibly comfortable, the need to control such quantities of fabric requires skill and dedication.

Above Hanging loose: baggy street fashion from the 1990s.
Left Delphos dress by Fortuny, 1906.

Right and below right
Lumps and Bumps
collection by Georgina
Godley, 1986.
Below Wooden corset by
Hussein Chalayan, 1995.

fur and feathers

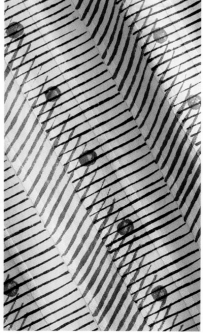

Above Block print by Susan
Bosence, and ploughed fields in
the Lincolnshire Wolds.
Left Heat-transfer print on indigo
cotton by Rebecca Earley.

fur and feathers

Right La Perse coat by
Paul Poiret, 1910.
Below Zebra print by
Dolce & Gabbana.

Printed textiles can depict nature by transferring
drawn images, by direct imitation of natural form, or
by abstracting from nature. Rebecca Earley's patterns
are made by transferring natural plant forms on to
indigo-dyed cotton, via the heat photogram process.
The actual plant, unmediated by drawing, is thus the
origin of the pattern. Susan Bosence (1913–96)
abstracted the landscapes of Devon and south-west
France into simple repeat patterns, in this instance
inspired by low sunlight on ploughed fields. A zebra
fabric by Dolce & Gabbana is a disguise to get noticed
in. Paul Poiret's La Perse coat uses block-printed fabric
by the painter Raoul Dufy. With its simple flower and
leaf shapes, drawn with a natural casualness and
precision, the garment still has the power to astonish.

Texture in nature derives in part from practical considerations, particularly the requirements of surface cooling and the absorption and release of moisture. For this purpose, a smooth, flat surface is less useful than a grained or wrinkled one, which has a greater surface area in relation to the size of the object it covers. Thus, the elephant's wrinkled skin helps it to remain cool, while fur is warm because it traps body heat and keeps out wind-chill. A surface may also be textured because of the renewal of the outer skin, as in the bark of certain trees that peels away to reveal new growth underneath. Issey Miyake has led a revolution in the development of fabrics as the basis for fashion design, mixing the natural and the artificial in what has been described as 'a system strictly designed for overthrowing the existing regulations'. Lainey Keogh's rippling dress for Autumn/Winter 1998 is reminiscent of human hair, both in the quality of the fabric and the way it has been designed. While fluffiness normally has connotations of feminine weakness, Fendi's crow-black shaggy coat suggests that feathers, too, can have attitude.

Above Jacket by Issey Miyake.
Right Fur makes a functional trimming for Inuit clothing.
Far right Wrinkled skin of the African elephant.

Left Dress by Lainey Keogh,
Autumn/Winter 1998.
Below Coat by Fendi,
Autumn/Winter 1998.

fur and feathers

Opposite Gucci catwalk
show, Autumn/Winter 1997.
Left Detail of Lady
Amherst's pheasant
(*Chrysolophus amhertiae*).
Below Diesel Style Lab
range, 1999.

Colour and texture are essential aspects of the
language of dress for which nature provides a wide
range of choices, none of which is essentially more
'natural' than another. Bright colours and subdued
ones operate in nature to satisfy different requirements,
so that the plumage of Lady Amherst's pheasant,
Chrysolophus amhertiae, is more gloriously arrayed
than Lady Amherst herself could ever have been.
Clothes correspond to different human situations.
We might seek attention through bright colours, with
Gucci's winter coats with their feathery texture, or
through the rugged 'natural' look of Diesel's Style Lab
range, where the 'wild nature' photographic background
to the fashion shoot contributes to the buyer's
understanding of the meaning of the clothes. In reality,
of course, these clothes are far from being a form of
outdoor camouflage; they are intended to show up
against a contrasting background of artificiality, and to
confer a moral quality of 'naturalness' on the wearer,
perhaps making him feel at ease in a wider variety of
social situations than he might wearing more formal
clothes or less carefully differentiated casual ones.

'On her neck the small face buoyant, like a bell-flower on its bed,' wrote the Victorian poet Robert Browning of a certain ideal of female beauty. Hats are worn less often today than in his time, but this has not prevented designers from developing the analogy between the human head and the flower on its stem, or the many kinds of cresting found in birds and animals. The designer Philip Treacy here uses magnificent swooping curves to give the effect of kinetic sculpture, cutting arcs through space. If hats are exceptional wear, shoes are essential and tend increasingly to be shaped by function and comfort rather than by fashion. Three extreme examples seen here apply imagery from nature to achieve a frisson of incongruity. The egg-and-chicken sandals by Camper are slyly inserted into a very 'whole-earth' range of footwear that promotes itself through the slogan 'Comfort with Imagination'. The 'hoof shoe', by Benoît Méléard in collaboration with Jeremy Scott, revives the Surrealist interest in shoes that make your toes tingle through their worrying incongruity. Wearing something of exaggerated size on your feet and ankles, like the model with the dog, emphasises a slender body and adds an element of burlesque humour to life.

Above Hat by Philip Treacy Autumn/Winter 1998.
Right Arum lily (*Zantedeschia aethiopica*).

Left Twins by Spanish shoe company Camper.
Right Hoof Shoe by Benoît Méléard in collaboration with Jeremy Scott.
Below Love me, love my dog.

Above Headdress of Lady Pu-abi, made of gold, lapis lazuli, carnelian and shell, Ur, Iraq, *c.*2650-2550 BC.
Left Pebble brooch designed by Ann Little.
Right Mah Rana's brooches made from butterflies and old wedding rings.

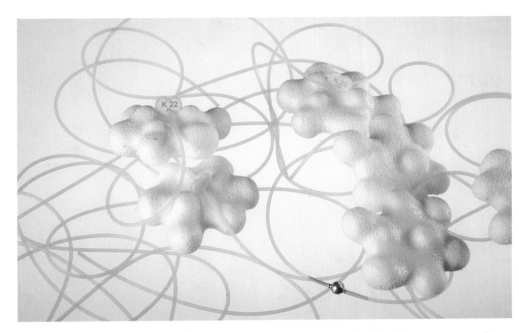

Left Christoph Zellweger's Commodity Chain K22.
Below Necklace by Dorothy Hogg.

The need for jewellery to catch the eye at a distance, while retaining visual interest at close range, reflects those features in the natural world, like flowers and pebbles, that reveal form patterns of increasing complexity as one approaches them. Jewellery functions in a wholly symbolic way, although its meaning is not necessary explicit. Jewellery from the earliest recorded western civilisations, such as the headdress of Lady Pu-abi, made in Ur, Iraq, four and a half thousand years ago, is not only astonishing in its beauty and craftsmanship but also startlingly modern in its simplification of natural form. The same effect of filigree delicacy is found in Mah Rana's reworkings of second-hand wedding rings to which butterflies are attached, or Christoph Zellweger's polystyrene jewellery, a material normally discarded but treated ironically as precious in the piece Commodity Chain K22. Ann Little's pebble brooch speaks of the simplicity of the found object from nature, while Dorothy Hogg's necklace seems to turn the body into a flower not by the customary device of depicting a flower, but by adding giant stamen-like forms.

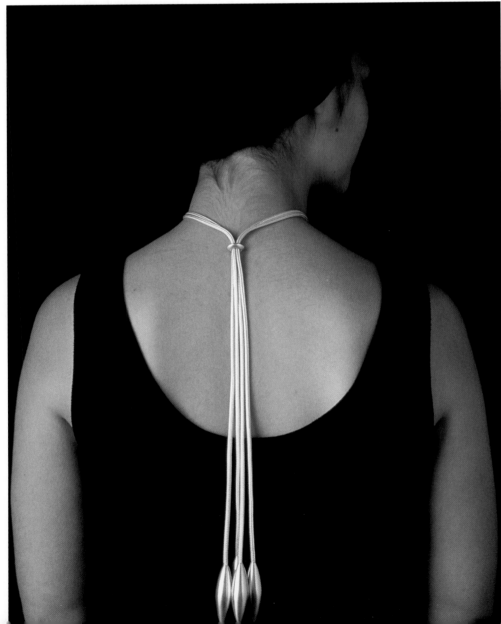

The skin has considerable scope as a 'canvas' for decoration, the meaning of which changes between cultures. Among the Mursi people of Ethiopia, body scarification is a means of attracting the opposite sex and records personal achievements, such as skill at hunting or outstanding bravery in battle. Tattooing imprints information about what a person is or aspires to be, and in western civilisations conveys the message of being in some way separate from normal society, or 'marked for life'. Thus tattooing becomes a sort of modern tribal cult, either devoted entirely to this symbolism of separateness, or indicating separation related to a special occupation – whether as a sailor, biker or Japanese gangster. Tattooing can also have a religious significance, celebrating the beauty of the body. The socially acceptable version of body painting, in western society, is make-up. The Versus range by Versace shows how, instead of emphasising the given patterns of the face, make-up can also create its own pattern, adding strong graphic lines which raise hidden responses to an undefined tribal significance.

Clockwise from top
Tattooed torso of Yazuka, Japanese gangster; temporary henna painting to celebrate Eid-ul-Fitr, Lahore, Pakistan; Versus make-up range by Versace; scarification, Mursi people.

133

fur and feathers

Graphic design uses nature in a great variety of ways. Signage has to catch the eye without confusing it, while photography and illustration select the images they need from the natural world and influence the way we look. Some products, such as films, advertising and packaging, have layers of meaning beyond the direct communication of information. In these cases, the subliminal messages not only relate to nature in terms of the psychology of perception but also touch people's aspirations for a different way of life or even for a better world.

We have to depend on the limitations and subjectivity of our human minds when considering the question of perception. How we see what we see, and the emotional effect that it has upon us, is

attraction and display

something we engage with every day. For the professional designer, a working knowledge of this area is a fundamental skill, often intimately related to the needs of industrial production. Indeed, much scientific research leading to a deeper understanding of nature has been motivated by the needs of industry.

designed to attract and to conceal

Poisonous creatures, such as wasps, tree frogs and snakes, often have skin brightly coloured in yellow or red, contrasted with areas of black, which singles them out as objects to be avoided by predators. Some reptiles move relatively slowly and would therefore be vulnerable when out in the open, so it is a good insurance policy for both parties that the predator avoids being poisoned by eating what otherwise looks like an easily available meal. Nature is not altogether consistent in giving these markings; in fungi, for example, while the fly agaric with its red cap and white spots looks, to the human eye, like something to avoid, the even more dangerous death cap mushroom exhibits no such obvious danger signs.

The designer of an orange and black warning sign has not necessarily been thinking about tree-frogs or wasps. However, the human eye evidently operates on the same principles of perceiving contrast that make these colour markings effective in the wild. Is there an atavistic memory of a primitive human condition that helps to make these colour combinations even more striking? They would certainly be almost intolerably stimulating to live with as everyday surroundings.

Previous page
The 'eye' on the hind wing of a Peruvian owl butterfly is designed to startle predators, distracting attention from the real, more vulnerable, head.
Right RMS Olympic in the dazzle camouflage adopted during the First World War in order to confuse German U-boats.

Camouflage operates in the opposite way to these marks of obvious presence. It creates confused outlines and colours that do not contrast strongly, offering a form of protection often used in nature by the predators themselves. Natural selection seems the most plausible explanation for such peculiarities as the imitation eyes found in the feather markings beneath the wing of the owl, which can be revealed suddenly to confuse a potential victim, or the 'eye' on the wings of the skate, which frightens predators on the ocean floor. There are also certain observed cases of adaptation to the environment, such as the moths that were seen to take on the colour and texture of the polluted industrial environment in which they lived. Where camouflage is used for human purposes, it relies on breaking down both the external form and the outline of the object by introducing curved lines and shapes and using a palette of colours drawn from the surrounding environment, whether it is woodland, desert, Arctic ice or ocean.

Military camouflage developed in earnest in the long-drawn-out and static warfare of the trenches in the First World War. Painters and stage designers were enlisted to help, among them Oliver Bernard, who later designed Art Deco restaurant interiors in London. They worked by trial and error to achieve the maximum invisibility. The British painter Norman Wilkinson (1878–1971) realised that, for ships, it was not enough to be invisible in order to avoid being hit by German submarines. It was necessary to confuse the enemy about the speed and direction of the ship, and for this purpose he devised the startling abstract geometry of 'dazzle camouflage', using a black and white contrast, rather like a zebra hide, to break up the mass of the ship. His countryman Edward Wadsworth (1889–1949) was one of ten lieutenants who carried out Wilkinson's designs in the shipyards, and later made paintings, prints and posters on this theme.

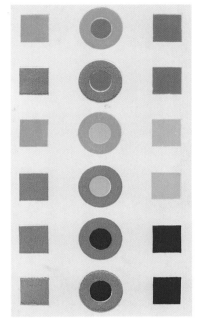

attraction and display

Above A diagram of colour relationships from M. E. Chevreul's book The Laws of Contrast of Colour, first published in 1839.

the psychology of vision

The great colour theorist of nineteenth-century France, M. E. Chevreul (1786–1889), was Director of the Dye Works at the Gobelins Tapestry Factory. He discovered that the secret to more intense colour was to be found not in stronger dyes, but in the perceptual capacity of the eye. Placing side by side colours selected carefully to complement and enhance each other, he achieved 'simultaneous contrast', by which one colour was modified by another and could be made to appear stronger. His theories were used by the Impressionists to see the world in a fresh way: not as a black and white image with added colour, as the academic painters had tended to see it, but as a fizzing and dissolving structure of brightness. The English translator of Chevreul's book, *The Laws of Contrast of Colour*, quoted a critic's opinion that 'to be familiar with this book is to possess a new sense. Every object in art and nature speaks a new and exciting language.'

The application of commonsense observation, rather than received wisdom, (a sort of 'Eureka!' factor, testified to in the lives of great inventors) underlay such nineteenth-century developments as dot screen colour printing – a process first suggested by the scientist Sir James Clerk Maxwell (1831–79) in 1861 and developed industrially in the United States in 1881. The eye cannot pick out the individual four-colour dots and mixes them optically into a complete range of colours. The system involved angling the dot screen through which the colours were separated (in different directions for each colour), so that dots of pure colour would act in contrast with each other rather than being mixed into a mud colour. This is the process – now more mechanically sophisticated, but essentially the same – by which the coloured pictures in this book are printed more than a hundred years later.

The relationship between colour and industrial design was first systematically explored by the Latvian-born colour theorist Wilhelm Ostwald (1853–1932), a Nobel Prize winner for physical chemistry in 1909. The previous year, some German industrialists had formed the Deutsche Werkbund, with the intention of improving the aesthetic quality and technical efficiency of all German products. Ostwald worked with them to produce a standard colour range according to his theory that the spectrum includes eight hues, based on four primary colours, adding green to the normal triad of yellow, red and blue as a fundamental colour. The reason for codifying colours in this way was mainly to enable precise specification and colour-matching, but also to encourage a more creative use of harmonious colour.

The Russian painter Wassily Kandinsky (1866–1944) laid some of the theoretical foundations of abstract art in his book *Concerning the Spiritual in Art*. These included matching certain colours to geometric forms, so that yellow, a keen colour, is seen as a sharp form, such as a triangle; while blue, being soft and deep, is round. Kandinsky brought these ideas to the teaching programme of the Bauhaus in Weimar when he joined it in 1921. Red became reserved for the square. The Swiss painter Johannes Itten (1888–1967), the first master of the *Vorkurs* or preliminary course at the Bauhaus, published his book of colour theory in 1961, claiming that nature provided most of the associational feeling about colour, particularly in relation to the colouring of the different seasons. Thus he wrote: 'The youthful light, radiant generation of nature in spring is expressed by luminous colours. Yellow is the colour nearest to white light, and yellow-green is its intensification ... Yellow, pink and lilac are often seen in the buds of plants.'

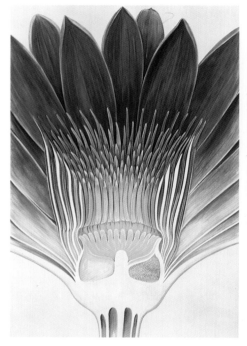

attraction and display

nature illustrated

Our way of seeing nature is unavoidably influenced by its portrayal through drawing and photography. Even when the intention is to inform, as in botanical illustrations, the image cannot fail to have an aesthetic impact. Here, too, the tendency is to present the object, whether it is an animal or a flower, in isolation, even though it is really meaningful only in context in the wild.

Despite the development of photography, drawing remains the art form most commonly associated with botanical discovery. A small number of specialist artists still work closely with the major botanical collections to make record drawings in a traditional way. These serve best for the identification of the species and have not varied substantially since the herbals of the Middle Ages

Above The Cape blue waterlily, painted by Arthur Henry Church in 1907.
Right Nature photograph by Ernst Haas, featured in his book Creation.

and their successors among early printed books. They involved a conscious level of design in selecting the way that the plant is displayed, whether symmetrically on the page or more 'naturally'. Some of these drawings are magnificent works of craftsmanship, engraved on copper and coloured by hand; they are not only accurate but also elegant, and show reverence for the plants concerned. The copper plates engraved to record the flora of the South Pacific, discovered on the voyages of James Cook in the 1780s, were so expensive that Sir Joseph Banks, the aristocrat-naturalist who commissioned them, went bankrupt and a complete edition of the images was not published until 200 years later.

They can also have a kind of humour, like an individual portrait. As the English romantic artist Samuel Palmer (1805–81) wrote: 'All the very finest original pictures, and the topping things in nature, have a certain quaintness by which they partly affect us; not the quaintness of bungling – the queer doings of a common thought; but a curiousness in their beauty, a salt on their tails, by which the imagination catches hold on them.' In the cheaper medium of wood engraving, the English illustrator Thomas Bewick (1753–1828) faithfully illustrated *British Birds and Quadrupeds* in black and white, adding his humorous tailpieces and vignettes that tell us so much about country life in the age of Constable and Wordsworth.

Until quite recently, botanical illustration was preferred to photography for books, because better colour could be obtained. Popular books of the 1940s, such as those published by Insel Verlag in Germany, the King Penguins in England that imitated them, and the Puffin Picture Books series intended for children, all had drawn illustrations of very high quality. Illustrators have more liberty than photographers to add their own emotional message to the image. Thus, animals can be presented, especially to children, in a number of ways, emphasising their closeness to humans in some cases, and their quality of strangeness and ferocity in others.

Photography, however, has been equally important in showing the manifold reality of nature. The tradition of botanical illustration influenced the way that subjects were often shown on a blank background. The German photographer Karl Blossfeldt (1865–1932) began his career as an industrial designer in an iron foundry at Magdeburg in the 1880s, and photographed plants to prove that natural forms were inherently reproduced in art. His work began at the time of Art Nouveau, but was later seen as a forerunner of Die Neue Sachlichkeit (the New Objectivity), which was the term adopted in Germany for the Modern Movement in the 1920s. Blossfeldt's commentary to the second volume of *Art Forms in*

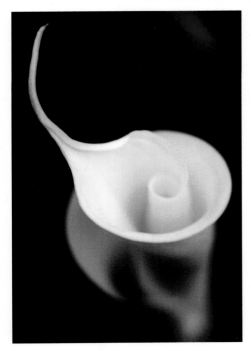

Nature, published in the year of his death, 1932, gives a Darwinian view of adaptation and survival in nature as an analogy for functionalism in design: 'The plant may be described as an architectural structure, shaped and designed ornamentally and objectively. Compelled in its fight for existence to build in a purposeful manner, it constructs the necessary and practical units for its advancement, governed by the laws familiar to every architect, and combines practicability and expediency in the highest form of art.' The modernists who admired his pictures found Blossfeldt's rhetoric too close to Nazi propaganda. In the work of American photographer Imogen Cunningham (1883–1976), close-ups of flowers assume a different meaning to Blossfeldt's, less to do with form and more suggestive of sexuality. The German photographer Andreas Feininger, whose father taught at the Bauhaus, published *The Anatomy of Nature* in 1956, which continues the essentially nineteenth-century wonderment at the forms of nature and their importance as a source of functional form. His revised edition, *Form in Nature and Life* (1966), and the 1977 book, *The Mountains of the Mind*, combine their visual delight in nature with anxious environmentalist texts – a symptom of the speed with which the thinkers of the western world were confronted with the evidence of impending ecological disaster.

Photographs have almost become our standard of truth about nature, but they are always the result of the photographer's selection of subject and manipulation of image. The results can make nature appear threatening or fragile, as well as beautiful in many different moods. Their two-dimensionality can neither reproduce the true visual experience of being in nature, nor the evidence of the other senses such as sound and touch, which produce a deeper sense of awareness in the presence of living things. Nevertheless, photographs can serve as a reminder of such sensations. Photography can also reveal things that the eye cannot see. William Henry Fox Talbot (1800–77), the Englishman who was one of the inventors of photography in the 1830s, included direct contact reproductions of leaf forms among his earliest experiments, soon progressing to taking microscope photographs (known as photomicrographs) of butterflies' wings and sections through the stems of plants. Images of this kind were unlike anything produced by botanical illustrators, having a strangeness owing nothing to human intervention. The images inspired artists such as the French symbolist Odilon Redon (1840–1916), who wrote in 1909: 'It is only after making an effort of will to represent with minute care a blade of grass, a stone, a branch, the face of an old wall, that I am overcome by the irresistible urge to create something imaginary.'

The same excitement was felt among the first generation of modern artists and designers, particularly in the practice of photography at the Bauhaus. It was subsequently transmitted into advertising, graphic design and textiles, such as those designed in the 1950s by the British sculptor

Above Nature idealised in a 1930s advertisement for Dunlop tyres.

Eduardo Paolozzi (1924–), using black and white abstract imagery. In the 1990s, the imagery of science is no longer black and white. Images are usually coloured, and actual photographs from nature, particularly when used for design purposes, usually favour the brightest colour contrasts. It could be said that nature already has a tendency to advertise built into it.

nature sells

Modern industry and commerce are usually identified as the cause of environmental problems. They, more than anything else except the global financial institutions on which they depend, have the ability to put things right. Environmental organisations such as Greenpeace and Friends of the Earth have been successful in using the media to highlight companies or governments that they believe to be guilty; as a result, it has become important for the latter to establish green credentials. Company reports, advertisements and posters all work subliminally to make associations in our minds between such enterprises as oil companies, nuclear fuel and mineral extraction on one hand, and images of happy people, clear skies and unpolluted water on the other. Ecology has thus achieved a graphic style of its own and become part of our cultural furniture. All the skills of designers are needed to prevent it from becoming over-familiar at a time when there is growing awareness, but no cause for complacency. In product and packaging design, certain well-developed motifs are supposed to indicate 'green' and 'nature'. For the most part, these rely on nostalgia through Bewick-style wood engravings of animals and countryside, bright flat colours like 1930s railway posters or textured, brown surfaces that indicate 'hand-made; expensive but pretending to be cheap'.

Where consumers can choose between products, the evidence shows that they favour things that they know will be environmentally beneficial. Some companies have made a special feature of their eco-friendliness, notably the British-based toiletries company The Body Shop, which has moved herbal remedies from the margins of commerce to become part of everyday shopping. One of their simple ideas was to provide refills of their liquid products in the customer's own bottles, since many people feel guilty about the number of containers they have to buy, even if these are capable of being recycled. Similarly, in 1990, the huge Danish supermarket, Irma, banned PVC packaging from their stores, setting up their own programme to research alternatives. In Denmark, a great beer-drinking country, no cans are allowed – only glass bottles that can be recycled, as was common for milk bottles in England and wine bottles in the Mediterranean until the 1970s. More recently, the Lammbrau brewery in Neumarkt, Germany, has promoted a beer made from organically grown ingredients, dried where necessary by solar power and sold in bottles intended for recycling, with no disposable metal foil around the neck. In Germany, where cans are sold, every second one is recycled.

Ecology has a novelty value in the marketplace and the current minimalist trend in design responds to the idea of living simply, perhaps with an excessive emphasis on a puritan look. Sometimes the products sold with a 'green' ticket are cheap, but equally often their simplicity is targeted at a sector of the market which prefers the exclusivity of paying more to be different. Producers and retailers have the choice whether to keep 'green' products as a profitable sideline, or to make a complete change in their priorities and offer these goods to the mass market.

wanted: careful owners for nature

In 1968, a dozen members of the 'Yippie' movement (the Youth International Party) in the United States went into the visitors' gallery of the New York Stock Exchange and threw money on to the brokers below. This was a spontaneous gesture, in the nature of a sixties 'happening', which attracted considerable press attention. Abbie Hoffman, speaking for the Yippies, declared of his newfound form of imaginative protest: 'We would hurl ourselves across the canvas of society, like streaks of splattered paint. Highly visual images would become news, and rumourmongers would rush to spread the excited word.'

In a similar spirit of anti-establishment activism, a group of Canadians tried in 1971 to sail a ship to the Pacific Island of Amchitka to 'witness' a controversial American nuclear bomb test. This was the origin of Greenpeace, a group based on the Quaker idea of 'bearing witness' by making peaceful protests and awakening the world to a sense of responsibility. Their methods, which have been consistently successful in embarrassing governments and large companies, depend on the mainstream media, and they soon discovered ways of getting front-page coverage by setting up photogenic events.

Greenpeace's campaign against wearing fur has changed perceptions almost universally. It was stimulated in 1985 by a sixty-second film by the famous contemporary British fashion photographer David Bailey, which subverted the form of a fashion show by showing blood spurting out of a fur coat and on to the audience. This generated the billboard poster with the caption: 'It takes 40 dumb animals to make a fur coat. But only one to wear it.' Such skilful manipulation of the media shows the power of images, although it also invites the accusation that in playing the 'media game', campaign groups are colluding with newspapers and television companies – which, after all, are only interested in selling more of their own product. The image of retreat from civilisation, the 1960s ideal of an 'alternative' culture, has been replaced by Greenpeace's paradigm of going to the scene of the problem and creating awareness.

In a political climate where it is necessary to be seen to be 'green', it is not difficult for multinational companies to portray themselves in a positive light through the use of a softer kind of imagery of nature. The rise of public relations consultancies and the practice of 'spin' mean that the shock tactics of Greenpeace and other campaigning groups may find it more difficult to catch their opponents napping. Sometimes, the real enemy is not so much the multinational company or irresponsible government as a sense of apathy closer to home and less easily categorised. The limited success of green parties in politics is testimony to the fact that, deep down, other priorities may rank more highly.

The legacy of the 'design culture' of the 1980s may seem to be an increase in consumerism, which makes only limited gestures towards a concern for the environment. However, it is now becoming clearer how the process of designing consumable products might be diverted away from its destructive tendency and towards goals of sustainability, by improving quality and durability. Designers cannot do more than try to lead their immediate clients and end-users increasingly into the paths of virtue by an awareness of the consequences of their actions. It is interesting to read the highly politicised thoughts of Philippe Starck, who in 1996 contradicted the image that some might hold of him as a designer of style-obsessed objects: 'How can those who act in the name of economies ignore that equilibrium is now world-wide? ... That we have to show solidarity on a world-wide scale, if not for reasons of morality and civilisation, then simply for the sake of survival of the species? ... On my own modest level, I am trying to ponder it out. But everyone should be pondering, asking themselves questions about life, money, desire, war, themselves. The profession of designer is one which is very closely linked to these changes. The designer can and should participate in the search for meaning, in the construction of a civilised world.'

Yellow and black say 'Danger'. The high level of contrast between these colours is visible to the human eye just as it is among animal species. An insect or reptile with this kind of coloration is conspicuous for reasons of self-protection: its predators become aware that to attack or eat such a creature will result in a sting or at least an unpleasant taste, and possibly poisoning after eating. The common wasp uses sound as well as sight as a warning, while the contrasting colours become most conspicuous when in motion, the time when such creatures are most vulnerable. Black also contrasts strongly with red and with orange, colorations equally found in nature, as in the Mexican red-leg tarantula, with its orange and black striped legs. Similar colour contrasts are used in traffic signs and notices alerting people to dangerous situations. These have a verbal and graphic content, but also communicate subliminally through colours which people are predisposed to respond to as danger signs. Nature protects itself by physical means, too, through barbs and sharp points that look threatening and serve to warn off an investigative approach by a hostile outsider.

Clockwise from top
Don't mess with wasps; a wasp-coloured Stop sign; beautiful but not cuddly: a Mexican cactus from Isla San Benito photographed by Peter Maschkan; an unmistakable warning sign; bright and dangerous, the Mexican red-leg tarantula.

attraction and display

Above John Leigh-Pemberton,
illustration for Shell, 1948.
Below Thomas Bewick, 'Fox', from
General History of Quadrapeds, 1790.

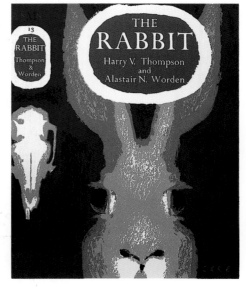

Left and below Clifford
and Rosemary Ellis,
sketch and book jacket
from *The Rabbit*, 1956.

Left Joachim Camaerarius
the Younger, Sunflower,
from *Florilegium*, c.1590.
Below Arthur Rackham,
'In the Forest with a Barrel',
from *Rip Van Winkle* by
Washington Irving, 1905.

Illustration forms many of our ideas about nature,
from Peter Rabbit onwards. Botanical illustrators
convey information, but rarely without adding some
interpretation that reveals their own time, as seen
in the splendid Baroque flourish of Camaerarius's
sixteenth-century sunflower. Thomas Bewick's wood
engravings of birds and animals were drawn from direct
observation, and often have moralistic or humorous
undertones. Attention to detail akin to Bewick's is
found more than a hundred years later in the series of
illustrations by John Leigh-Pemberton, used as
advertisements for Shell petrol and motor oil. A more
visually and conceptually challenging interpretation of
nature comes from the book jackets by Clifford and
Rosemary Ellis for the Collins New Naturalist series,
begun in 1945. Sketches were translated into designs
that went well beyond sentimental portrayal. Arthur
Rackham's illustration for *Rip Van Winkle* is one of
many in which he portrayed the threatening quality
of trees, in a way that was to influence subsequent
generations of animated film designers.

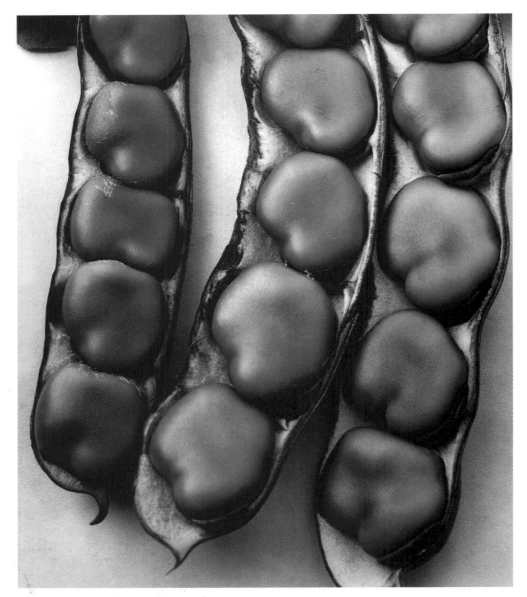

Photography, a medium that sometimes claims to be impersonal and objective, has done much to influence concepts of nature since its invention in the 1830s. Charles Jones photographed the vegetables which he grew as a professional gardener for purposes far removed from art, but his recently rediscovered negatives reveal an intense, almost surrealistic, concentration on abstract form and its other-worldliness. Karl Blossfeldt's images of nature, by contrast, were intended to inspire designers. The delicate flower photographs of Imogen Cunningham emphasise a feminine quality of softness and secrecy. Landscape, which reveals the interrelated ecological systems in nature, is a more difficult subject to show in a single image. The eye may interpret it as abstract form or, with sufficient knowledge, see the evidence of change over time as clearly as in a speeded-up film.

attraction and display

Clockwise from top
Magnolia flower by Imogen
Cunningham; alienation in
landscape: Monument
Valley, USA, by Simon
Marsden; pumpkin
(*Cucurbita pepo*)
photographed in hard-
edged isolation by Karl
Blossfeldt; detail of cactus;
broad beans in their pods
by Charles Jones.

EVERYWHERE YOU GO

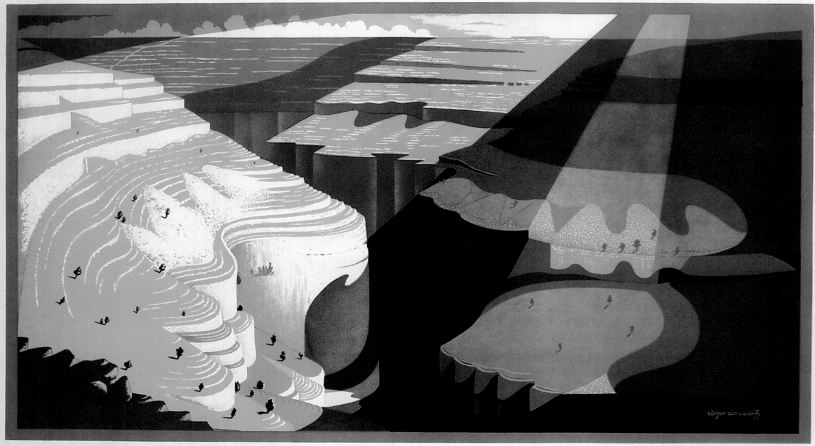

GORDALE SCAR - THE CRAVEN FAULT, YORKS.   EDGAR AINSWORTH

YOU CAN BE SURE OF SHELL

LOOK NO FURTHER.

ESSO PRICEWATCH

Clockwise from top
'Goredale Scar', poster for
Shell, by Edgar Ainsworth,
1934; 'Cool as a mountain
stream': Consulate
cigarettes enjoying a
country outing in the 1960s;
'Silvikrin goes natural':
one of the most widely
advertised brands of
shampoo in the 1960s;
Esso poster *c.*1998.

Printed advertising frequently uses images drawn from
nature to validate products and services. In the 1920s,
Shell began to advertise petrol in terms of places to
visit in Britain, giving the brand an association with
intelligent tourism as well as security. Today, motorists
are subjected to all kinds of subliminal messages to
persuade them to buy a particular brand of petrol, and
Esso's 1960s' tiger (who came with the catchphrase
'Put a tiger in your tank') has been redeployed to stress
value for money. Nature as a reference is increasingly
used by advertising to create an effect of surprise or
humour, but products relating to the body often seek a
more basic association with nature to assert their
quality and lack of harmful ingredients. Tobacco is
a product of nature, one of many whose benefits to
mankind are hard to ascertain. Menthol cigarettes
were launched on somewhat spurious associations
with wild mountain streams and the healthy outdoors.

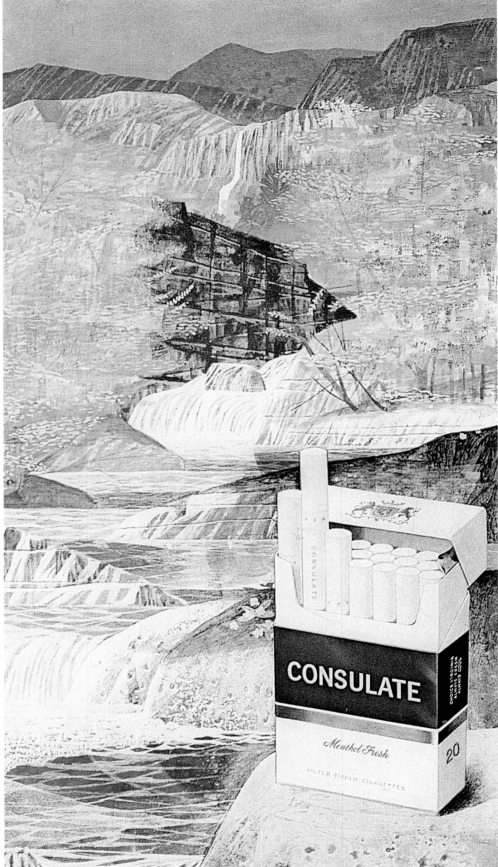

Gröna Konsums
Miljörapport 1997

Clockwise from left Cover
for Gröna Konsums annual
report, photograph by Eva
Wernlid/Tiofoto,1997; Muji
refill packs and CD holder,
1999; bottles for Neal's Yard
Remedies, 1999.

In the jungle of retailing, companies like to make their
products distinctive and appealing. Environmentalism
may be a passing fashion but it has created a minimalist
chic, partly based on Japanese precedents. Muji,
makers of unbranded, undecorated household and
office equipment, are a notable example of the dressed-
down style, whether for hair-product refills or for a
cardboard CD holder. These designs are comparable
to Philippe Starck's packaging for rice – it is the
opposite of 'ethnic' style. Crabtree & Evelyn has always
excelled in packaging design for toiletries and gift
foods, and the company's recent designs, by illustrator
Laura Stoddart, are the latest in a distinguished line.
Brown glass bottles and old-fashioned labels give the
appeal of ancient wisdom to herbal remedies from
Neal's Yard. Shop interiors have to match the mood of
the products, and a sparse look – more like an art gallery
– is an automatic signal of refinement. Companies
compete to acquire a green image, and the annual report
of Swedish supermarket chain Gröna Konsums uses an
evocative, film-like image of nature and culture.

Clockwise from top Browns
Living shop interior, South
Molton Street, London;
organic rice packaging by
Philippe Starck for Lima,
1998; packaging for
Crabtree & Evelyn by
Laura Stoddart, 1999.

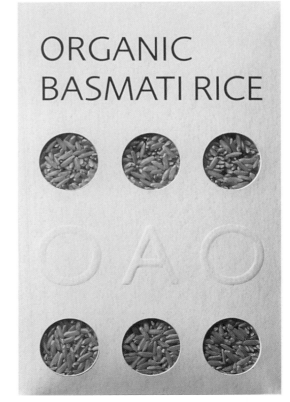

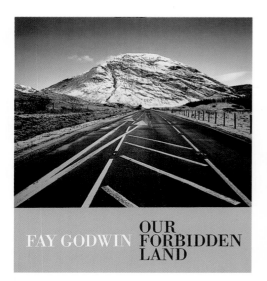

FAY GODWIN   OUR FORBIDDEN LAND

Clockwise from far left
'May Day' poster, 1987;
cover of *Our Forbidden
Land* by Fay Godwin, 1990;
Friends of the Earth poster;
Greenpeace poster.

Wild Places Under Threat !

You can help protect them

Graphic design is a powerful tool for changing opinion about the environment. It can charm, like Common Ground's 'May Day' poster, issued in 1987 as a full-page newspaper advertisement to launch a campaign for local distinctiveness; the campaign has since been adopted as government policy. Fay Godwin's photographs in *Our Forbidden Land* (Jonathan Cape) were part of a campaign for increased public access to the countryside; part of the aim was to expose pollution and the destruction of nature. Greenpeace has made environmental action into something of an art form, setting up newsworthy photos such as this projection onto a cooling tower. Friends of the Earth, a British-based organisation, launched its appealing image of 'wild places under threat' to emphasise the limited opportunities for children to enjoy nature at the end of the twentieth century.

atmosphere under threat

STOP DO, GO SOLAR

STOP CLIMATE CHANGE!

GREENPEACE

GREENPEACE
Environmental Trust

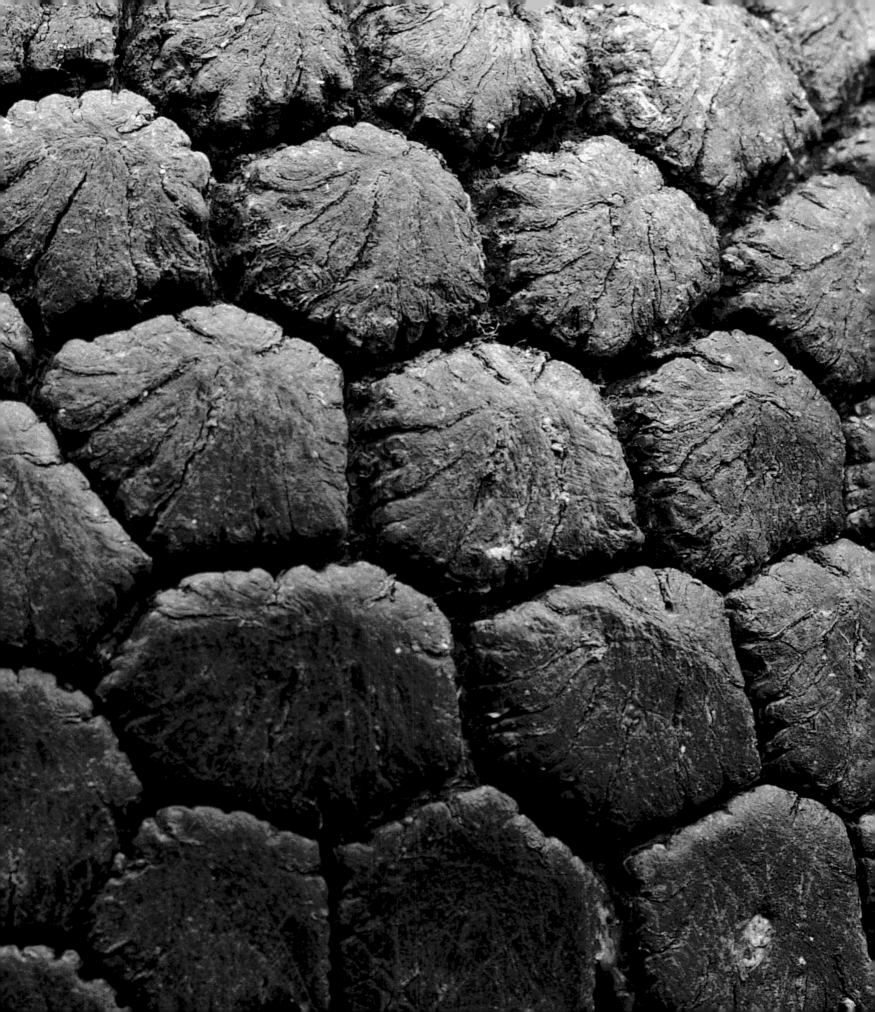

Abram, David, *The Spell of the Sensuous*, New York, Vintage Books, 1997

Alexander, Christopher, *The Timeless Way of Building*, New York, Oxford University Press, 1979

Aristotle, translated by Robin Waterfield, *The Physics*, Oxford, Oxford University Press, 1996

Barnes, Jonathan, ed., *Early Greek Philosophy*, Harmondsworth, Penguin Books, 1987

Barrow, John D., *The Artful Universe: The Cosmic Source of Human Creativity*, London, Penguin Books, 1997

Bateson, Gregory, *Mind and Nature: A Necessary Unity*, London, Wildwood House, 1979

Bayes, Kenneth, *Living Architecture: Rudolf Steiner's Ideas in Practice*, Edinburgh, Floris Books, 1994

Beukers, Adriaan, and Ed van Hinte, eds, *Lightness*, Rotterdam, 010 Publishers, 1998

Blake, William, *Blake: Complete Writings*, ed. Geoffrey Keynes, London, Oxford University Press, 1966

Blier, Suzanne Preston, *The Anatomy of Architecture: Ontology and Metaphor in Batammaliba Architectural Expression*, Cambridge, Cambridge University Press, 1987

Bortoft, Henri, *The Wholeness of Nature: Goethe's Way of Science*, New York, Lindisfarne Press / Edinburgh, Floris Press, 1996

Buck, Alex, and Helen Clifford, *Out of this World: The Influence of Nature in Craft and Design 1880–1995*, London, Crafts Council, 1995

Buddensieg, Tilmann, *Industriekultur: Peter Behrens and the AEG*, Cambridge, Mass. and London, MIT Press, 1984

Capra, Fritjof, *The Tao of Physics*, London, Wildwood House, 1975

————, *The Turning Point*, New York, Simon & Schuster / London, Wildwood House, 1982

————, *The Web of Life*, London, Harper Collins, 1996

Carson, Rachel, *Silent Spring*, New York, Houghton Mifflin, 1962

Chermayeff, Serge, and Alexander Tzonis, *The Shape of Community: Realisation of Human Potential*, Harmondsworth, Penguin Books, 1971

Clifford, Sue, and Angela King, eds, *Local Distinctiveness: Place Peculiarity and Identity*, London, Common Ground, 1993

Cook, Theodore Andrea, *The Curves of Life*, London, Constable & Co., 1914

Coomaraswamy, Ananda, *Traditional Art and Symbolism*, ed. Roger Lipsey, New Jersey, Princeton University Press, 1977

Croall, Stephen, and William Rankin, *Ecology for Beginners*, Duxford, Icon Books, 1992

Crowe, Norman, *Nature and the Idea of a Man-made World*, Cambridge, Mass. and London, MIT Press, 1995

Day, Christopher, *Places of the Soul: Architecture and Environmental Design as a Healing Art*, London and San Francisco, Thorsons, 1995

Day, Lewis F., *Nature and Ornament*, London, B. T. Batsford Ltd, 1908

Descartes, Réné, translated by John Cottingham, Robert Stoothoff and Dugald Murdock, *The Philosophical Writings of Descartes*, Cambridge, Cambridge University Press, 1985

Dickens, Peter, *Reconstructing Nature: Alienation, Emancipation and the Division of Labour*, London and New York, Routledge, 1996

Drabbe, Natascha, ed., *Refuse: Making the Most of What We Have*, Utrecht, Cultural Connections, 1997

Eck, Caroline van, *Organicism in Nineteenth-century Architecture*, Amsterdam, Architettura & Natura Press, 1994

Farmer, John, *Green Shift: Towards a Green Sensibility in Architecture*, Oxford, Architectural Press, 1996

Feininger, Andreas, *Forms in Nature and Life*, London, Thames & Hudson, 1966

Gleick, James, *Chaos: The Amazing Science of the Unpredictable*, London, William Heinemann Ltd, 1988

Goldin, Owen, and Kilroe, Patricia, eds, *Human Life and the Natural World: Readings in the History of Western Philosophy*, Ontario and New York, Broadview Press, 1997

Gombrich, Ernst, with Max Black and Julian E. Hochberg, *Art, Perception and Reality*, Baltimore and London, Johns Hopkins University Press, 1972

Goody, Jack, *The Culture of Flowers*, Cambridge, Cambridge University Press, 1993

Gordon, J. E., *Structures, or Why Things Don't Fall Down*, London, Penguin Books, 1978

Gould, Stephen Jay, *Life's Grandeur*, London, Vintage Books, 1997

Hawken, Paul, *The Ecology of Commerce: A Declaration of Sustainability*, London, Weidenfeld & Nicolson, 1994

Heathcote, Edwin, *Imre Makovecz: The Wings of the Soul*, Chichester, Academy Editions, 1997

Hitchmough, Wendy, *C. F. A. Voysey*, London, Phaidon Press, 1995

Jackson, John Brinkerhoff, *Discovering the Vernacular Landscape*, New Haven and London, Yale University Press, 1984

Jacobs, Jane, *The Death and Life of Great American Cities*, New York, Vintage Books, 1961

Jencks, Charles, *The Architecture of the Jumping Universe*, London, Academy Editions, 1995

Jenger, Jean, *Le Corbusier: Architect of a New Age*, London, Thames & Hudson, 1996

Kandinsky, Wassily, translated by Michael Sadler, *Concerning the Spiritual in Art*, New York, Dover Publications, 1977

Kauffman, Stuart, *At Home in the Universe: The Search for Laws of Self-organisation and Complexity*, London, Penguin Books, 1996

Keeble, Brian, *Art: For Whom and for What?*, Ipswich, Golgonooza Press, 1998

Kepes, Georgy, *The New Landscape in Art and Science*, Chicago, Paul Thobald & Co., 1956

Koren, Leonard, *Undesigning the Bath*, Berkeley, Stone Bridge Press, 1996

Leslie, C. R., *Memoirs of the Life of John Constable*, London, Phaidon Press, 1951

Loos, Adolf, *Spoken into the Void: Collected Essays 1897–1900*, introduction by Aldo Rossi, Cambridge, Mass. and London, MIT Press, 1982

Lovejoy, Arthur O., *The Great Chain of Being: A study of the History of an Idea*, Cambridge, Mass., Harvard University Press, 1936

Lovelock, James, *Gaia: A New Look at Life on Earth*, Oxford, Oxford University Press, 1979

Lucretius, translated by R. E. Latham, *The Nature of the Universe*, Harmondsworth, Penguin Books, 1951

Lurie, Alison, *The Language of Clothes*, London, Bloomsbury, 1992

Mann, Margery, *Imogen Cunningham Photographs*, Seattle and London, University of Washington Press, 1970

Michell, John, *The Earth Spirit: Its Ways, Shrines and Mysteries*, London, Thames & Hudson, 1975

Miele, Chris, ed., *William Morris on Architecture*, Sheffield, Sheffield University Press, 1996

Murphy, Pat, *By Nature's Design*, San Francisco, Chronicle Books, 1993

Needham, Joseph, *The Grand Titration: Science and Society in East and West*, London, George Allen & Unwin, 1969

Oliver, Paul, *Encyclopedia of Vernacular Architecture of the World*, Cambridge, Cambridge University Press, 1997

Papanek, Victor, *Design for the Real World*, London, Thames & Hudson, 1972

————, *The Green Imperative: Ecology and Ethics in Design and Architecture*, London, Thames & Hudson, 1995

Pearce, Peter, *Structure in Nature is a Strategy for Design*, Cambridge, Mass. and London, MIT Press, 1978

Plato, translated by H. D. P. Lee, *Timaeus and Critias*, Harmondsworth, Penguin Books, 1965

Plotinus, translated by Stephen McKenna, *The Enneads*, London, Penguin Books, 1991

Poulson, Christine, *William Morris on Art and Design*, Sheffield, Sheffield University Press, 1996

Pound, Ezra, *The Pisan Cantos*, London, Faber & Faber, 1949

Rudofsky, Bernard, *Are Clothes Modern?*, Chicago, Paul Theobald, 1947

Ruskin, John, *Ruskin Today*, ed. Kenneth Clark, London, John Murray, 1964

Sacher-Masoch, Leopold von, 'Venus in Furs', in *Masochism*, New York, Zone Books, 1991

Schivelbusch, Wolfgang, *Disenchanted Light: The Industrialisation of Light in the Nineteenth Century*, Oxford, Berg Publishers, 1988

Sheldrake, Rupert, *A New Science of Life*, London, Blond & Briggs, 1981

Sherrard, Philip, *The Rape of Man and Nature: An Enquiry into the Origins and Consequences of Modern Science*, Ipswich, Golgonooza Press, 1987

Starck, Philippe, *Starck*, ed. Simone Philippi, Cologne and London, Taschen Books, 1996

Stevens, Peter S., *Patterns in Nature*, Boston, Mass., Little, Brown & Co., 1974

Taylor, Frederick Winslow, *The Principles of Scientific Management*, New York, Harper & Bros, 1914

Thompson, D'Arcy Wentworth, *On Growth and Form*, Cambridge, Cambidge University Press, 1961

Toulmin, Stephen, *Cosmopolis: The Hidden Agenda of Modernity*, Chicago, University of Chicago Press, 1990

Vogel, Steven, *Life's Devices: The Physical World of Animals and Plants*, New Jersey, Princeton University Press, 1988

————, *Cats' Paws and Catapults: Mechanical Models of Nature and People*, New York and London, W. W. Norton & Co., 1998

Weston, Richard, *Alvar Aalto*, London, Phaidon Press, 1995

White, Daniel R., *Postmodern Ecology: Communication, Evolution and Play*, Albany, State University of New York Press, 1998

Wilde, Ann and Jurgen, eds, *Karl Blossfeldt: The Alphabet of Plants*, New York, te Neues Publishing Company, 1997

Williams, Raymond, *Keywords*, London, Fontana, 1976

bibliography

index

index

This book has been the work of many hands and I would particularly like to thank Stuart Cooper, who commissioned it, and the staff of Conran Octopus who helped to give it shape. As picture researcher, Ally Ireson made a significant contribution to the development of its themes.

I am grateful to Arnold Rattenbury and Shoestring Press for their permission to print the poem 1887: Willow Boughs, from the book Morris Papers, 1996.

My colleagues at the Prince of Wales's Institute of Architecture over the last seven years have introduced me to ideas that have helped me understand the subject in greater depth. My wife Susanna has, as always, provided a sounding-board for ideas as they emerge from the jungle, as well as more practical support than any author has the right to expect.

The publisher would like to thank the following photographers and organizations for their kind permission to reproduce the photographs in this book:
1 Ines Roberts/Flowers & Foliage; 3 Anthea Simms; 5 Bruce Iverson/Science Photo Library; 6-7 Julian Cotton Photo Library/Jason Hawkes Aerial Collection; 8 H Schafer/SOA; 9 Adam Hart-Davis/Science Photo Library; 10 David Cavagnaro; 11 George Steinmetz/Katz Pictures; 12-13 Angelo Hornak; 14 Birds Portchmouth Russum; 15 Richard Glover; 16 AKG London; 17 Devonshire Collection, Chatsworth. By permission of the Duke of Devonshire and the Chatsworth Settlement Trustees; 19 Martin Charles; 20 Claude Nuridsany/Science Photo Library; 21 Archipress; 22 Getty Research Institute, Los Angeles/DACS London 1999; 24 George Steinmetz/Katz Pictures; 25 Ken Gibson/Wildlife Matters; 27 Max Plunger; 28-29 Heather Angel; 30 NOAA/John Wells/Science Photo Library; 31 above Kathie Atkinson/Oxford Scientific Films; 31 below Heather Angel; 32 The Science Museum/Science & Society Picture Library; 33 Peter Menzel/Science Photo Library; 34 Claude Nuridsany/Science Photo Library; 35 D Roberts/Science Photo Library; 36 David Cavagnaro; 37 Jim Brandenburg/Robert Harding; 38 Richard Glover; 39 Science Photo Library; 40 Peter Cook/View; 42-43 Tim Griffith/Esto; 44 Francois-Xavier Bouchart/Archipress; 45 above Frans Lanting/Robert Harding; 45 below Richard Glover; 46 John Ormerod/Ancient Art & Architecture; 47 Martin Jones/Arcaid; 48 Richard Bryant/Arcaid; 49 Imagination (courtesy Nicholas Grimshaw & Partners Ltd); 50-51 Images Colour Library; 50 below left Carl R Sams II/Still Pictures; 50 below right CORBIS/Ken O'Brien Collection; 51 below Brian Jacquest/The Special Photographers Library; 52 Timothy Hursley; 53 above Paul Raftery/Arcaid; 53 below centre László Sáros; 53 below right SEA Studios/Photonica; 54 above Alan Weintraub/Arcaid; 54-55 Michael Freeman; 55 above left The Architectural Association/Tim Street-Porter; 55 above right Edifice/Darley; 56 above left Heather Angel; 56 above right Richard Bryant/Arcaid; 56 below Richard Bryant/Arcaid; 57 Ezra Stoller/Esto; 58 left Jussi Tiainen; 58 right Chris Sattlberger/Panos Pictures; 59 above left Bernhard Schmid/Photonica; 59 below left Katsuhisa Kida; 59 right Mark Fiennes/Arcaid; 60 Michael Freeman; 61 above left Charles Aithie/Ffotograff; 61 above right CORBIS/Craig Aurness; 61 below left The Architectural Association/Ludwig Abache; 61 below right Richard Barnes; 62 Lars Hallen; 63 Lars Hallen; 64 above Mandy Reynolds ABIPP; 64 below Benson + Forsyth; 65 above Ross Honeysett; 65 below Tim Street-Porter; 66 above Dennis Freppel/Archipress; 66 below left James Morris/Axiom; 66 centre David Curl/Oxford Scientific Films; 66-67 Richard Glover; 67 above left Professor Harold Egerton/Science Photo Library; above right Imagination; below right John Edward Linden/Arcaid; 68-69 Hiroyuki Hirai; 70 The National Trust Photographic Library/Ian Shaw; 71 Richard Glover; 73 Tony Stone Images; 74 Private Collection/Accademia Italiana, London/Bridgeman Art Library; 75 Deidi von Schaewen; 76 above Peter Cook/View; 76 below left Alan Weintraub/Arcaid; 76 below right Peter Cook/View; 77 Bill Tingey/Arcaid; 78 Julius Schulman; 79 above Alan Weintraub/Arcaid; 79 below left Peter Aaron/Esto; 79 below right Sotheby's Picture Library, London; 80 above Deidi von Schaewen; 80 below left Peter Cook/View; 80 below right Chris Gascoigne/View; 81 Lars Hallen (Jukka Siren); 82 left Pascal & Maria Marechaux; 82 right Edifice/Lewis; 83 above left Deidi von Schaewen; 83 centre Nathan Willock/View; 83 above right Michael Freeman; 83 below David Churchill/Arcaid; 84-85 Janis Hall; 84 below left Edifice/Darley; 84 below right Richard Waite/Arcaid; 85 ©Chris Drury (from his book Silent Spaces, Thames & Hudson 1998); 86 above Lucinda Lambton/Arcaid; 86 below Carlos Dominguez/Casa de Marie Claire; 87 above Deidi von Schaewen; 87 below The Local History Unit, Enfield Libraries; 88 World of Interiors/Simon Upton; 89 above left Vivian Russell; 89 above right Edwin Smith; 89 below Edifice/Darley; 90 above left Peter Cook/View; 90 above right CORBIS/Michael Busselle; 90 below Nicholas Kane/Arcaid; 91 above Peter Aaron/Esto; 91 below left Deidi von Schaewen; 91 below right Kari Haavisto; 92 above Ben Van Den Brink/Still Pictures; 92 below Deidi von Schaewen; 93 above Katsuhisa Kida; 93 below Richard Harrington; 94-95 Lon van Keulen (Interior magazine No.13); 96 Shannon Tofts; 97 The National Trust Photographic Library/Jonathan Gibson; 99 Michael Freeman; 100 Christie's Images Ltd; 101 Victoria & Albert Museum, London, UK/Bridgeman Art Library; 102 above Amazed (Madeleine & Dudley Edwards); 102 below left Natalie Woolf, Surface Design, Leeds; 102 below right David Parker/Science Photo Library; 103 above Jim Holmes/Axiom; 103 below Christie's Images Ltd; 104 above Victoria & Albert Museum, London, UK/Bridgeman Art Library; 104 below The Whitworth Art Gallery, The University of Manchester ('Effects' by Heath, 1959); 105 Metropolitan Museum of Art, New York, USA/Bridgeman Art Library; 106 World of Interiors/Annabel Elston; 107 above Christie's Images Ltd; 107 below left Christoph Kicherer; 107 below right Earl Carter/Belle/Arcaid; 108 above The Science Museum/Science & Society Photo Library; 108 centre Aqua Creations/Catalytico; 108 below left Mark Fiennes; 108 below right Linda Burgess/The Garden Picture Library; 109 Ingo Maurer Gmbh/Catalytico; 110 Iitala Glass, Finland; 111 above left Kate Malone; 111 above right The Dartington Pottery; 111 below World of Interiors/Jonathan Lovekin; 112-113 MMT coll. UFAC, Paris; 114 Steve Turner/Oxford Scientific Films; 115 Topham Picturepoint; 117 Mary Evans Picture Library; 118 Chris Parker/Axiom; 120 left MMT coll. UFAC, Paris; 120 right Ralph L Blair/PYMCA; 121 left Anthea Simms; 121 above right Cindy Palmano; 121 below right Cindy Palmano; 122 left Rebecca Earley; 122 above right Susan Bosence/The Crafts Council; 122 below right P Wilson/SOA; 123 left P Biasion/Vogue France/Conde Nast/MMT coll. UFAC, Paris; 123 right Mike Fear (courtesy private collector); 124 above left Sigurd Kranendonk/Eigenhuis & Interieur; 124 below left CORBIS/Library of Congress; 124 below right Planet Earth Pictures/Steve Bloom; 125 left Anthea Simms; 125 right P Biasion/Vogue France/Conde Nast/MMT coll. UFAC, Paris; 126 Anthea Simms; 127 above David Cavagnaro; 127 below Rankin; 128 above Anthea Simms; 128 below Ines Roberts/Flowers & Foliage; 129 above left Camper; 129 above right Frank magazine; 129 below Andrew Lamb; 130 above University of Pennsylvania Museum (neg. T4-28c); 130 below left Ann Little/John McGregor/The Crafts Council; 130 below right Edward Barber; 131 above Christoph Zellweger; 131 below Dorothy Hogg/John McGregor/The Crafts Council; 132 Carol Beckwith & Angela Fisher/Robert Estall Photo Agency; 133 above Sandi Fellman (courtesy Jane H Baum Gallery, New York); 133 below left Cannonieri & Fortis; 133 below right Trip/Viesti Collection; 134-135 Sinclair Stammers/Science Photo Library; 136 The Imperial War Museum; 138 The Natural History Museum, London, UK/Bridgeman Art Library; 139 Ernst Haas/Hulton Getty; 140 The Advertising Archives; 142 above left Tony Stones Images; 142 above right Images Colour Library; 142 below left Tony Stone Images; 142 below right N A Callow/Robert Harding; 143 David Cavagnaro; 144 above The Advertising Archives; 144 below left Mary Evans Picture Library; 144 below centre courtesy Peter Marren; 144 below right courtesy Peter Marren; 145 left Christie's Images Ltd; 145 right The Fine Art Society, London, UK/Bridgeman Art Library; 146 above CORBIS/Sean Sexton Collection; 146 below left Millennium/Peter Maschkan; 146 below right Karl Blossfeldt Archiv, Ann and Jurgen Wilde, Zulpich/DACS London 1999; 147 above Christie's Images Ltd; 147 below The Marsden Archive, UK/Bridgeman Art Library; 148 above Christie's Images Ltd; 148 below The Advertising Archives; 149 left The Advertising Archives; 149 right The Advertising Archives; 150 above left courtesy of Grona Konsums, Sweden; 150 above right Muji; 150 below left Neal's Yard Remedies; 150 below right Muji; 151 above James Bedford/Browns Living (Nathalie de Leval/Andrew Jones); 151 below left Crabtree & Evelyn; 151 below right Agence Starck; 152 courtesy Common Ground; 153 above left courtesy Fay Godwin; 153 below left courtesy Greepeace; 153 right courtesy Friends of the Earth; 154-155 David Cavagnaro

Every effort has been made to trace the copyright holders, architects and designers and we apologise for any unintentional omission and would be pleased to insert the appropriate acknowledgement in any subsequent edition.

author's acknowledgements and picture credits